take up
SOFT FURNISHINGS

Take up
SOFT FURNISHINGS

SUE WHITING

MEREHURST

Published in 1995 by
Merehurst Limited
Ferry House, 51-57 Lacy Road,
Putney, London SW15 1PR

ISBN 1–85391–450–9

A catalogue record of this book is
available from the British Library.

Edited by Heather Dewhurst
Designed by Kit Johnson
Photography by Di Lewis
Illustrations by Paul Bryant

Typesetting by
Litho Link Limited, Welshpool, Powys

Colour separation by
Fotographics Ltd, UK – Hong Kong

Printed in Italy by Milanostampa SpA

CONTENTS

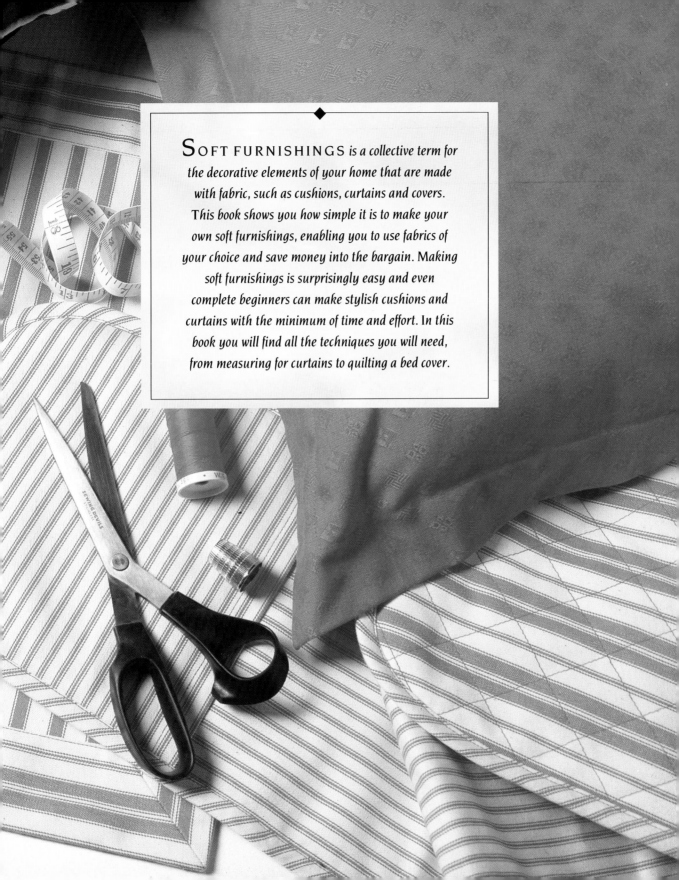

SOFT FURNISHINGS *is a collective term for the decorative elements of your home that are made with fabric, such as cushions, curtains and covers. This book shows you how simple it is to make your own soft furnishings, enabling you to use fabrics of your choice and save money into the bargain. Making soft furnishings is surprisingly easy and even complete beginners can make stylish cushions and curtains with the minimum of time and effort. In this book you will find all the techniques you will need, from measuring for curtains to quilting a bed cover.*

CUSHION COVERS

*Cushion covers are really easy to make
and, if the fabrics used to make them coordinate with the
furnishings already in the room, the effect they create can be
quite stunning!*

Cushion pads

Ready-made cushion pads are widely available in a variety of sizes and shapes. They basically fall into two groups – gusseted and un-gusseted. **Un-gusseted pads** are where two pieces of fabric of exactly the same size and shape are joined and filled – like a pillow. **Gusseted pads** are where another strip of fabric is used to join together the two shaped pieces. This can be a wide strip used to join two small circles to make a long, thin sausage-shaped bolster cushion, or a long, thin strip joining two bigger circles to form a circular, cake-like cushion.

Regardless of whether the cushion is gusseted or not, the shape of the main side pieces can vary – they can be square, rectangular, circular or any fancy shape you like – but the way the cushion cover is made is basically the same.

Covers for un-gusseted pads

These are the simplest of all types of covers. Start by making a pattern of the shape of one side of your cushion pad. If the pad is square or rectangular, measure the sides and draw a square or rectangle of that size onto a sheet of paper. If it is circular, draw a circle of the correct diameter onto your paper.

As you will be seaming the two sides together, you will need to add a seam allowance around the outer edges. For most types of fabric, 1.5cm (⅝in) should be sufficient but, if the fabric you are using frays very easily, a seam allowance of 2cm (¾in) will help to stop the seam pulling apart.

Once you have your pattern piece, fold your chosen fabric in half and cut out this shape twice. Neaten the raw edges of the cut fabric shapes now by zigzag stitching by machine over the raw edges. With the right sides of the two fabric pieces together, sew the two sections together along the edges. If the cover is square or rectangular, leave one side open to insert the pad and pivot your stitching at the corners. If the cover is circular, leave an opening the same size as the diameter of the cushion pad.

Turn your cover right side out and insert the cushion pad. Fold in the seam allowance along the opening and slip stitch these edges together by hand.

Covers for gusseted pads

Make your pattern for the sides and for the gusset strip. For a square or rectangular cushion pad, the length of your gusset strip should be the same as the length of all four finished sides of your pad plus two seam allowances. For a circular pad, it should be the circumference of the circle plus two seam allowances. The width of the strip should be the depth of the gusset plus seam allowances on both sides.

From your fabric, cut out two side pieces and one gusset strip. Join the ends of the gusset strip together and press this seam open. If the pad is square or rectangular, mark the corner points of the side sections along the edges of the gusset strip. Join each of the side pieces to the gusset, leaving an opening. Turn the cover right side out, insert your pad and slip stitch the opening closed.

UN-GUSSETED COVER

◆ Machine stitch the two side pieces together along all edges, taking the correct seam allowance. If the cover is square or rectangular, pivot the stitching at the corners. Stop stitching at the corner point with the needle in the fabric, raise the machine foot and turn the work. Lower the foot to continue. Work a few stitches in reverse at each end of the seam, where the opening to insert the pad begins and ends.

SQUARE GUSSETED COVER

◆ If you are making a square or rectangular gusseted cover, mark the corner points of the sides along the edges of the gusset strip. Stitch along the edge, just within the seam line, near these corner points and then make a cut into this stitching line at the exact corner point. When you come to join the gusset strip to the sides, open out this cut as you pivot the work to sew around the corner.

CIRCULAR GUSSETED COVER

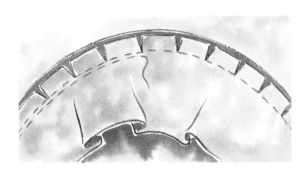

◆ If the cushion cover is a circular gusseted cover, stitch along the edges of the gusset strip just within the seam line. Make cuts into the stitching line all along the edge, leaving a distance between the cuts of about 3–5cm (1¼–2in). As you sew the gusset to the side sections, open out these cuts to allow you to join the two edges smoothly.

SLIP STITCHING THE OPENING

◆ Once the cushion cover has been turned through to the right side and the cushion pad inserted, turn in the seam allowance along the opening edges. Hand sew the opening closed by slip stitching the two folded edges together. Make sure you take small stitches to ensure the seam does not gape, and fasten off the thread ends securely.

Making cushion covers easily removable

It is highly likely that, from time to time, you will want to remove your cushion covers to launder them. You will find it much easier and quicker to do if the cushion cover has a proper opening, rather than if you have to un-pick and re-sew the hand-stitched seam. A zipped opening is the obvious answer.

The length of the zip is also very important – too short a zip will mean the pad is virtually impossible to get in and out. If you are using a square pad, the zip should be just shorter than the length of one side. If the pad is rectangular, the zip needs to be just shorter than the shorter edge. For a circular cushion, the zip needs to be the same length as the diameter of the circle.

The type of zip you choose depends on the fabric you are using and how much rough handling the cushion will receive. While a nylon zip is soft, flexible and washes well, it does have a tendency to burst open if, for example, a child jumps onto the cushion! A strong metal zip will withstand the rough and tumble of young children much more easily. As a basic rule, use nylon zips for covers that are made from lighter weight fabrics and where the cushion will be more decorative than practical, and use a metal zip for heavier fabrics and cushions that are going to have a lot of use.

The positioning of the zip opening will depend on the type of cushion cover you are making. If it is a plain cover, the opening can simply be inserted in one of the seams. However, if you are intending to use piping cord around the edge of the cover, or add some other sort of decorative detail in the seam, it will be easier to insert the zip elsewhere.

POSITIONING A ZIP OPENING

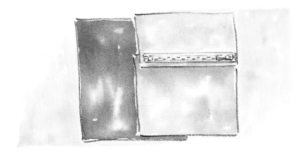

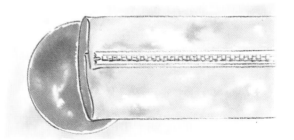

◆ If the zip opening is to fall across the back of the cushion, you will have to allow seam allowances along the opening. When making your pattern for the cover, decide where the opening is to be and make another pair of pattern pieces for this side of the cover, allowing seam allowances along the zip opening edges. From your fabric you will then cut out one full side piece and two part side pieces.

◆ If the cushion cover is gusseted and the gusset is quite wide – such as for a bolster cushion – the ideal place for the zip opening is along the seam in the gusset. You already have seam allowances added along these edges so you do not need to allow more.

INSERTING A ZIP

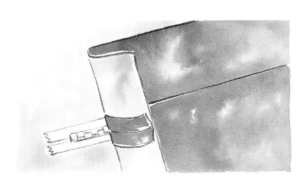

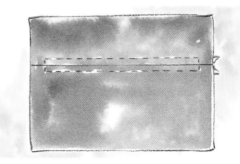

1 ◆ Start by tacking (basting) the seam along the edge where the zip will be so that the seam does not gape open. Press the seam open and carefully position the zip directly under the seam, with the right side of the zip against the wrong side of the fabric. If the zip is slightly shorter than the edge, machine stitch the ends of the seam, making sure that the seam is secure at both ends of the opening.

2 ◆ Tack (baste) the zip in place and, using a zip foot attachment on your machine, machine stitch the zip in place, stitching from the right side and in a rectangle so that both ends of the zip opening are secured. Remove the tacking (basting) stitches and complete the cover. There is no need to leave an opening in the seam as the zip can be unzipped and this opening used to turn the cover through.

Decorative details

While plain cushion covers in matching or toning fabrics are very effective, adding extra detail to the cushion cover can create wonderful effects. Adding piping around the edges of a cover is the classic finishing touch. Alternatively, inserting a frill into a cushion cover seam creates a soft and pretty look. You can create a dramatic studded effect by adding buttons to your covers. Cover a pair of self-cover buttons with fabric to match your cushion cover, and stitch them on both sides of the cover. These buttons will have to be removed to launder the cover.

Create a more textured surface to your cushion cover by lightly quilting it. As quilting has a tendency to 'shrink' the fabric, it should be quilted before the section is cut to size. Your quilting lines can follow the outline of the design on the fabric or can simply be parallel lines.

Adding a frill around a cover

Decide how wide you want your frill to be, remembering to add a narrow hem allowance to the outer edge and a seam allowance along the inner edge. To create a luxurious frill, the strip cut for the frill should be at least twice the length of the seam it is to be inserted into. Cut out your strip, or strips, of fabric for the frill, remembering to add seam allowances to the ends.

Making a frill as shown opposite will mean that, from one side, the wrong side of the fabric will show on the frill. If you are using a lightweight fabric, cut the strip twice the desired depth plus two seam allowances. Join the strip(s) and then fold it in half along its length with the wrong sides together. Tack (baste) the raw edges together and press the strip flat. The outer folded edge will form the outer edge of your frill and, as both sides of the frill are the right side of the fabric, the cover will look just as good from both sides!

PIPING A CUSHION COVER

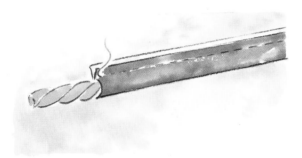

1 ◆ Buy sufficient piping cord to run all along the seam it is to be inserted in, allowing about 5cm (2in) for the join. From the remaining cover fabric, cut and join bias strips of fabric that are wide enough to wrap around the cord, plus two seam allowances. Wrap the bias strip snugly around the cord so that the right side shows and the two long edges match, and tack (baste) the strip in place right next to the cord.

2 ◆ Lay this piping strip onto the right side of one of the cover side pieces, positioning the tacked (basted) line along the cover seam line, and tack (baste) it in place, stitching along the previous tacking (basting) line. Where the two ends meet, overlap them, running the cord out towards the cut edge. At the corners of a square or rectangular cover, snip into the piping fabric seam allowance to open it out to go around the corner. Lay the second cover side piece onto the first and stitch together, stitching exactly along the tacked (basted) line. Use a zip foot attachment so you can stitch right up against the edge of the cord.

1 ◆ Join the ends of the strip(s) together to create a circle of fabric and press the seams open. Make the narrow hem around the outer edge. Using a long machine stitch, run two rows of gathering threads along the other edge, positioning the lines of stitching on either side of the seam line.

2 ◆ Pull up the gathering threads to the length of the seam the frill is to be inserted into and lay your frill against the right side of one side of your cover. Pin and tack (baste) the frill in place, distributing the gathers evenly. Allow extra fullness at the corners so that the frill will lie flat. Sew the sides of the cover together, with the frill in between. Then remove the tacking (basting) and gathering threads.

ADDING BUTTONS

QUILTING A COVER

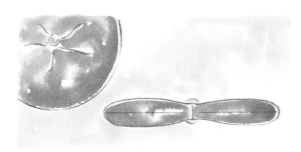

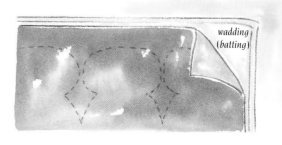

wadding (batting)

◆ Insert the pad inside the cushion cover and close the opening. Using strong thread (such as that designed for attaching buttons) and positioning the two buttons directly opposite each other, one on each side, sew the two buttons in place, stitching right through the cushion from one side to the other. Pull up the thread tightly so that the cushion is pulled in and fasten off the thread very securely.

◆ Cut out a piece of cover fabric, a piece of polyester wadding (batting) and a piece of fine backing fabric, all larger than the finished size of the cover. Sandwich the wadding (batting) between the two fabric pieces and tack (baste) them together. Quilt the fabrics by machine stitching through all the layers, working from the right side of the cover fabric. Then lay your pattern piece onto the quilted section, cut it out and make up your cover in the usual way.

CUSHION COMFORT

These cushion covers mix prints and plain fabrics
to create a soft but sophisticated look. Although at first glance they
look complicated, all these covers are surprisingly easy to make —
and there's not a zip in sight!

Bolster cushion cover will fit pad 46cm (18in) long, with an end diameter of 18cm (7in). Square piped cushion covers and cushions with borders will fit 43cm (17¼in) square pad.

YOU WILL NEED

Bolster cushion cover

65cm (26in) fabric, 137cm (54in) wide

140cm (56in) narrow piping cord

50cm (20in) snapper tape

Matching thread

Both square cushions

50cm (20in) fabric, 137cm (54in) wide

190cm (76in) narrow piping cord

Matching thread

Square cushion with piping & button

Oddment of contrasting print fabric

1 self-cover button

Matching thread

Cushion with border

60cm (24in) fabric, 137cm (54in) wide

Matching thread

Cushion with double border

60cm (24in) plain fabric, 137cm (54in) wide, for front

70cm (28in) print fabric, 137cm (54in) wide, for back

Matching thread

BOLSTER CUSHION COVERS
(*shown in blue print*)

1 ♦ From the fabric, cut a rectangle measuring 63cm (25¼in) by 49cm (19½in) for the side, and two end circles 21cm (8⅜in) in diameter. Turnings of 1.5cm (⅝in) are included. From the remaining fabric, cut 4cm (1½in) wide bias strips and join these to form one length of 140cm (56in).

2 ♦ Wrap the bias strip around piping cord and stitch in place close to the cord. Trim the turnings of the strip to 1cm (⅜in) and cut the strip into two equal lengths. Pin and tack (baste) each piping strip to the right side of each end circle, positioning the previous stitching line of piping 1.5cm (⅝in) in from outer edge and with raw edges of piping facing towards raw edges of circles. Overlap ends of piping cord and run them out towards the outer edge of the circle.

3 ♦ Along one shorter edge of the side piece, fold 1.5cm (⅝in) to the wrong side. Fold the same amount to the *right* side along the opposite edge. Unfasten the snapper tape and lay half over each of the two raw edges, positioning the centre of the stud fasteners 1.5cm (⅝in) in from the folded edge. Check that the studs will match when fastened and that they do not fall within the end seam allowances. Then stitch in place along both edges. Fasten the tape and stitch across the ends of the tape through all layers of fabric.

4 ♦ Pin and tack (baste) the end pieces to the side and then stitch in place, stitching close to the piping cord. Unfasten the snapper tape and turn the cover through to the right side. Insert the cushion pad.

SQUARE PIPED CUSHION
(*shown in terracotta*)

1 ♦ From the fabric, cut one piece measuring 46cm (18in) square for the front, and two pieces measuring 46 × 30cm (18 × 12in) for the back. Turnings of 1.5cm (⅝in) are included. From the remaining fabric, cut 4cm (1½in) wide bias strips and join these to form one length of 190cm (76in).

2 ♦ Wrap the bias strip around the piping cord and stitch in place close to the cord. Trim turnings of strip to 1cm (⅜in). Pin and tack (baste) the piping strip to the right side of the front, positioning previous stitching line of piping 1.5cm (⅝in) in from outer edge and with raw edges of piping facing towards raw edges of front. Snip into the piping strip turnings at the corners. Overlap the ends of piping cord and run them out towards the outer edge.

3 ♦ Fold 2cm (¾in) to the wrong side along one longer edge of each back piece. Turn under raw edge and stitch in place. Overlap finished edges of back pieces by 16cm (6⅜in) to form a 46cm (18in) square and stitch along side edges.

4 ♦ With right sides together, stitch back sections to front, enclosing piping in seam. Trim corners, turn through to right side and press. Insert cushion pad.

SQUARE CUSHION
WITH CONTRAST PIPING
AND BUTTON

(shown in blue, trimmed with blue print)

1 ◆ Follow steps 1 to 4 of the square piped cushion, but using print fabric for bias strips to cover the piping cord.

2 ◆ Cover the self-cover button with the same fabric as the piping strip. Using very strong thread (or at least four strands of polyester sewing thread), stitch the button centrally onto the front of the cushion, stitching right the way through the pad and out through the back of the cover, pulling up the thread tightly to pull the cushion in.

(NB: The button will have to be removed before the cover is removed for laundering.)

CUSHION WITH BORDER

(shown in blue, blue print and terracotta)

1 ◆ From the fabric, cut one piece measuring 53 × 120cm (21¼ × 48in). Turnings of 1.5cm (⅝in) are included.

2 ◆ Fold 2cm (¾in) to the wrong side along both shorter edges of the fabric. Turn under the raw edge and stitch in place. Press.

3 ◆ With right sides together, fold in one end of the fabric strip, folding 33cm (13¼in) from one end. Now fold the other end in the same amount to cover this first end – the distance between the folded edges should be 50cm (20in). Stitch across both side edges. Turn through to the right side and press, placing seams along pressed edges.

4 ◆ Working from the right side, stitch through all layers of fabric 3cm (1¼in) from all four edges to form a border. Insert the cushion pad.

CUSHION
WITH DOUBLE BORDER

(shown in blue with blue print)

1 ◆ From the plain fabric, cut out a 59cm (23½in) square for the front of the cover. From the print fabric, cut out a 67cm (26¾in) square for the border and front backing, and two rectangles measuring 47 × 35cm (18¾ × 14in) for the back cover sections. Turnings of 1.5cm (⅝in) are included in these measurements.

2 ◆ On the wrong side of the front piece, mark lines 4.5cm (1¾in) in from the outer edges. At each corner, fold the square diagonally with right sides facing so that the adjacent sides match. Then stitch across the corners at right angles to the folded edge, starting at the point where the two marked lines cross. Carefully trim away the excess fabric at the corners, leaving 1cm (⅜in) beyond the stitching line, and press these four mitred corner seams open. Turn the corners through to the right side and press again, pressing 4.5cm (1¾in) to the wrong side along all four edges.

3 ◆ Make up the backing piece in the same way as above but this time mark the lines 6.5cm (2½in) in from the edges and press this amount to the wrong side along all four edges once the section is turned through to the right side.

4 ◆ Lay the front backing piece flat with its wrong side facing uppermost. With the right side of the front section facing uppermost, lay this section centrally on top of the front backing piece – the backing section should extend 2cm (¾in) beyond the front section along all four edges. Tack (baste) the two sections together. Then, working from the right side, stitch the two pieces together along all four edges, stitching through all fabric layers 5cm (2in) in from the outer edge of the backing piece (3cm (1¼in) in from the edges of the front section). Press.

5 ◆ Fold 2cm (¾in) to the wrong side along one longer edge of each back section. Turn under the raw edge and stitch in place. Overlap the two finished edges of the back pieces to form a square measuring 47cm (18¾in) and stitch across the sides. Press 1.5cm (⅝in) to the wrong side along all four edges of this complete back section.

6 ◆ Lay the front pieces out flat with the front backing piece facing uppermost and lay the wrong side of the back sections on top of this. The edges of the back section should fall level with the previous stitching line. Tack (baste) the cushion pieces together just inside the pressed edges of the back sections.

7 ◆ Turn the complete cushion cover over and, working from the right side, stitch through all layers of fabric just inside the previous stitching line to secure the back of the cover to the front. Press. Insert the cushion pad.

Unlined Curtains

Making your own curtains can save a fortune –
but the idea of handling such large quantities of fabric
can be daunting! However, if a little care is taken, you will find
that curtains are surprisingly simple to make and the end
result is very rewarding. The secret to success is
calculating your fabric requirement correctly.

Choosing curtain fabric

Curtains are used for three reasons – to provide privacy, to keep in the warmth and to keep out the light. Depending on the window that the curtains are for, one of these reasons may be more or less important. For example, it is far more important to keep out the light in a child's bedroom than in a kitchen, but the main aim of a curtain in a living room or kitchen may be to retain privacy while allowing light in – hence the use of sheer, lace or net curtains. When selecting your curtain fabric, stop and think exactly what you want that curtain to do.

Most furnishing fabrics are suitable for use as curtains – the only real exceptions are the very heavy upholstery fabrics that are designed for covering furniture. If you are in any doubt about the suitability of the fabric you have chosen, ask the shop assistant for advice. When selecting fabric, bear in mind that, when the curtains are closed, there will be a very large expanse of fabric on view – a large bold print could overpower the rest of the room or, conversely, a busy pattern might appear too fussy in the wrong setting. Choose colours that complement your decor but don't be too conservative – a splash of colour can enliven a room considerably. Take into account, too, how often you are likely to want to launder your curtains and check whether the fabric is washable or needs to be dry-cleaned. Kitchen curtains, for example,

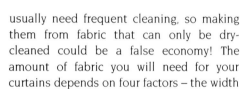

usually need frequent cleaning, so making them from fabric that can only be dry-cleaned could be a false economy! The amount of fabric you will need for your curtains depends on four factors – the width and type of track or pole they will be suspended from, the type of heading the curtains will have, the length the curtains will hang to and the size of the design repeat on your chosen fabric.

Curtain tracks and poles

It is possible that you may be making curtains to fit a pole or track already at a window. But, if not, have a look in a reputable hardware store at the wide variety of different curtain tracks and poles available. Each of the different sorts will create a different effect and most come complete with full details of exactly how they should be fixed in place. Once you have selected the one you want, check that you buy the correct size. Ideally, the track or pole needs to be wider than the window so that, when the curtains are opened, the curtain fabric will hang at the sides of the window, thereby allowing in as much light as possible. However, if the window is situated in an alcove or against an adjoining wall this may not be possible.

When your track or pole is in place, you can measure the finished width of your curtains. Some tracks have an overlapping section where the two curtains meet – this must be taken into account.

Heading tapes

Once you have established the finished width of each curtain when in place, you can start to calculate the actual fabric width for the curtains. The deciding factor here will be the type of heading tape you are going to use. This is the tape that is attached to the top of the curtain. Most heading tapes have threads or cords running through them that are pulled up to create different sorts of pleats or gathers. There will also be slots in the tape through which you thread the hooks that will be used to hang the curtain on the track or pole.

There is an almost endless variety to the types of pleats and gathers that can be created by the various tapes available and the one you choose will depend on the effect you want to create. While a feminine floral print will look even prettier with one of the fancy lattice gathering tapes across the top, grand living room curtains will look much more stately with a classic pencil-pleated heading.

Look carefully at the selection of heading tapes available and decide what effect you want to create. Remember that different types of tape use differing amounts of fullness in the curtain. A classic pencil-pleated tape will require the fabric width to be 2¼ to 2½ times the finished curtain width, some types of tape will only need the fabric to be twice as wide, while others may need three times the width. If you are not sure what amount of fullness your chosen heading tape requires, ask in the store – most manufacturers of curtain heading tape supply a printed guide to accompany their tapes.

Calculating the amount of fabric needed

At this stage, you know exactly how wide each finished curtain is to be and, obviously, it is highly unlikely that your chosen fabric will be this wide! You will need to join lengths of fabric to make up this width and now is the time to work out how many widths of fabric you will need for each curtain.

Divide the finished width of each curtain by the width of the fabric you have chosen and round this figure up to the nearest full (or half) width of fabric. Sometimes you may need a curtain to be, for example, 2½ times the width of the fabric. In these cases you will need to cut a fabric width in half along its length to give you this half-width. These narrower sections of fabric should be placed at the outer edges of the curtains, not in the centre where the two curtains meet.

For example, if each curtain is to hang at a finished width of 130cm (52in), and your chosen heading tape needs the fabric width to be 2½ times the curtain width, this makes the curtain fabric width 325cm (130in) (curtain width multiplied by required fullness of chosen tape). Your chosen fabric is 115cm (45in) wide. To calculate the numbers of widths of fabric you will need, divide 325cm (130in) (curtain fabric width) by 115cm (45in) (actual fabric width) and you get 2.8, which needs to be rounded up to 3. So you will need three widths of fabric for each curtain. (At this point, it is a good idea to jot down on a piece of paper how many widths of fabric you need so you don't forget!)

Any extra width you have in the fabric by rounding up to the nearest full (or half) width will normally be taken up by the hems down the sides and the seams joining the lengths. Any leftover fullness can usually be eased in when the heading tape is pulled up.

Now you have established how many widths of the fabric you need for your curtains, you must calculate how long each width needs to be, so that you can buy the correct amount of fabric.

In order to calculate the *length* of the curtain you need to decide where the lower edge of the curtain is to fall. Do you want the curtains to be full length, ending just above the floor? Or is the window in an alcove, meaning that the curtain must rest just above the windowsill? Where your curtain ends is purely a matter of personal taste and practicality.

Once you have decided on the position of the lower edge of the curtain, measure the distance between this point and the curtain track or pole. Use a metal ruler for this as fabric tape measures can stretch with frequent use, giving an inaccurate measurement. This measurement is basically the length of your finished curtain – but, onto this measurement, you must add a hem allowance at the bottom and an allowance at the top for the heading tape and turnings. An extra 20cm (8in) should be sufficient for both – any surplus can be trimmed away later. Make a note of this measurement now.

Now that you know how many widths of fabric you need and how long each width must be, you can work out how much fabric to buy. Multiply the number of widths needed by the length of each width to give you your total fabric requirement. Remember that you will more than likely be making a *pair* of curtains – so, if each curtain needs two widths, you will need a total of four widths for the pair.

In the previous example, we calculated we needed three widths of fabric for each curtain. For a pair of curtains, we will need six widths in total. The curtains are to be full length, ending about 3–4cm (1¼–1½in) above the floor, and the distance between the curtain track and this lower point is 237cm (94¾in). Add onto this measurement 20cm (8in) per length for hems and allowances, giving a length for each width of fabric of 257cm (102¾in). By multiplying the length of each width by the number of widths needed, we can establish we need to buy 1542cm (616¾in) of fabric – or 15.5m (17¼yd) when rounded up.

There is one other very important factor that will affect the amount of fabric you need to buy – the size of the repeat of the design on your chosen fabric. Obviously, with a plain fabric this need not be taken into account. But, if there is a printed or woven design on the fabric you will need to allow extra so that the design can be matched when the lengths are joined – in the same way as wallpaper strips are matched to the one they butt up against. Often you will find that the size of the design repeat is printed onto the fabric along the selvedge, along with the manufacturer's name. If it is not, look carefully at the fabric and measure it yourself. You need to allow one full pattern repeat for each fabric length over and above the first length. If you need four lengths of fabric for your pair of curtains, you must buy four times the required length *plus* three times the length of each pattern repeat.

In our earlier example, we established we would need 15.42m (17¼yd) of fabric for our curtains if we make them from a plain fabric. However, if we choose a fabric with a design on it, we could need a substantial amount more. We need six lengths of fabric

for our curtains, meaning we need to allow an extra five pattern repeats when buying the fabric. If the fabric we chose had a large pattern repeat of 60cm (24in), we would need to buy an extra 300cm (120in) – making the total amount of fabric go up to 18.5m (20⅔yd)! However, if we chose a fabric with a small repeat of just 10cm (4in), we would only need to allow an extra 50cm (20in) of fabric, so would just buy 16m (17⅔yd) – a difference of 2.5m (3yd). So you can see that it is important to bear in mind the size of the pattern repeat when selecting your fabric!

Preparing to make the curtains

Once you have calculated and bought your fabric you are ready to start to make your curtains. Before you begin, ensure you have everything you need – a working sewing machine, thread, sharp scissors, pins, ruler, chalk and, of course, heading tape. The amount of heading tape you need will be the same as the finished fabric width of each curtain, plus about 5cm (2in) per curtain for turnings at the ends.

Start by checking that your fabric is smooth, that there are no flaws in it and that one end is cut straight and at right angles to the selvedges. If it is not cut correctly, trim the end now. Ideally, you should cut straight across the grain by following the weave of the fabric – pull out a thread so that you have a guideline to follow as you cut. However, if you are using a printed fabric and the print does not exactly follow the grain of the fabric, cut the end straight following the line of the print, not the weave of the fabric.

Once the end is straight you can cut out your first length of fabric. On your piece of paper you have written down how many widths of fabric you need and the length of each width. Lay your fabric out flat on a firm surface – often a floor will be the only surface large enough. Now measure out your first length. Take care to measure correctly – if this one is wrong all the others will be wrong too! Using your chalk and your ruler, mark a line across the fabric at the correct distance from the straight end. Cut along this line and you have your first length.

Use this first length of fabric as a template for all the following lengths. Lay out more fabric from your roll and then lay this first length on top, making sure both pieces are smooth. If you are using a plain fabric, make sure the cut edges match and then cut your second length by following the other cut edge of the first length. If you are using a printed fabric, shuffle the first length along the roll so that the design matches perfectly along adjoining selvedges and then cut along both ends of your second length.

Continue in this way until you have the required number of cut lengths. If you are using a printed fabric, you may well have some fabric left over – this is due to the allowance you had to add to ensure you could match the pattern. Use it to make matching cushion covers (see page 9) or tie-backs (see page 36).

Making the curtains

Start by getting your sewing machine ready. As always when beginning a new sewing project, insert a new needle in your machine, ensuring it is the right size for the weight of fabric you will be sewing. Thread up the machine with matching thread – a synthetic thread is the best type to use as there is no risk of this type of thread shrinking when laundered and thereby creating puckered seams. Set up your machine to work a straight stitch of the correct length for the weight of fabric you are using. Most curtain fabrics are fairly heavyweight in comparison to dressmaking fabrics, so you will probably need a slightly longer stitch length than normal.

Seam the fabric lengths together, taking great care to match the design accurately as you go. Continue joining lengths of fabric to make up the size required for each curtain, stitching each seam in the same direction. After hemming the side edges of the curtain, you can then attach the heading tape (see page 22). You will first have to establish which end of the curtain will be the top edge – this is particularly important with printed fabrics! Then pull up the cords to gather the curtain to the correct width to fit the pole or track and knot the cords. Before hemming the lower edge of your curtains, it is a good idea to let the curtains hang for 24 hours as the weight of such a large expanse of fabric can make the curtains drop in length.

JOINING CURTAIN LENGTHS

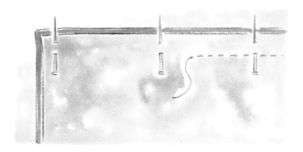

1 ◆ With the right sides of two fabric lengths facing, seam them together along one selvedge. If you are using a fabric with a design on it, take great care to match the design accurately. It may save time later if you pin and tack (baste) the seam before stitching it. Stitch the seam taking a seam allowance of about 2cm (¾in). However, you may find that the nature of the fabric along the selvedge, or design on the fabric, means you need to take a larger or smaller seam allowance than the usual one.

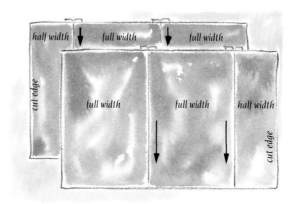

2 ◆ Continue to join the lengths of fabric to make up the size required for each curtain. Stitch each seam in the same direction. If you are using half-widths for your curtains, remember to cut one width in half parallel to the selvedges. These half-widths must be joined to the other sections along the selvedge, on the outer edges of the finished pair of curtains.

TRIMMING SELVEDGES

♦ The selvedges of most fabrics are often more tightly woven than the rest of the fabric and, if left intact, they could cause the curtain to pucker when it hangs at the window. To avoid this, if you are going to line the curtain, or re-neaten the edge, trim away a few millimetres of fabric along the selvedge or snip into the selvedge along each seam every 5cm (2in). Press all the seams open from the wrong side.

SEWING SIDE HEMS

♦ Trim away the selvedge along the side edges of the curtain and fold 3cm (1¼in) to the wrong side. Fold under the raw edge and hand stitch this second folded edge in place, taking care to ensure that the stitching does not show on the right side. If your fabric is very thick, you could neaten this cut edge rather than fold it under, thereby reducing the bulk. Press the side hems.

ATTACHING HEADING TAPE

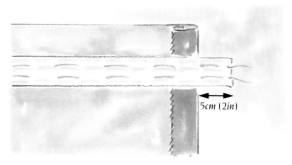

5cm (2in)

1 ♦ You are now ready to start to attach your heading tape. Before you begin, establish which end of each curtain will be the top edge – vitally important when working with prints! Measure the length of this upper edge and cut a length of heading tape to this measurement, adding about 5cm (2in) to the length to allow for turnings at each end.

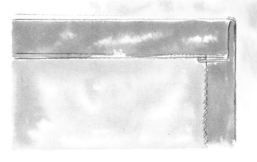

2 ♦ Fold the required amount of the curtain fabric to the wrong side across the top of each curtain. The amount you fold over will depend on how close you want the tape to be to the top edge of the curtain. If you are using a narrow heading tape and want the curtain to stand above the tape, creating a small frill, then you will obviously need to fold more to the wrong side than if the tape is to be placed right next to the upper edge of the curtain. However much you fold over, allow about 12mm (½in) of fabric to be hidden by the tape.

3 ◆ Lay the wrong side of the heading tape onto this end of the curtain so that one edge of the tape falls the required distance below the upper edge of the curtain. Fold under the ends of the tape so that these folded ends fall about 6mm (¼in) in from the side edge of the fabric. Pin and tack (baste) the tape in place on the curtain.

4 ◆ At each end of the tape, carefully pull the cords, or threads, that are used to pull up the tape from under the turnings. At one end – the end that will fall in the middle of the pair of curtains – knot these cord ends together securely. Leave the other cord ends free. These will be pulled up when the curtain is ready to be hung.

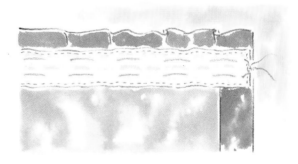

5 ◆ Stitch the tape in place along both long edges, stitching each edge in the same direction to avoid any distortion. Then stitch across the ends, ensuring that the ends of the cords are not caught in the stitching. Make sure that all the ends of the stitching are secured by working a few stitches in reverse. Press the upper edge of the curtain, working from the wrong side and taking care not to use too hot an iron – some curtain tapes will need a cooler iron than the fabric they could be sewn to!

6 ◆ Measure the length of the track or pole that the curtain is to hang along and then, very carefully, pull up the cords running through the heading tape until the upper edge of curtain matches this measurement. Knot the ends of the cord securely to hold the edge at this length. Do not cut off the ends of cord – you will need to release the cord when the curtain is laundered. The loose ends of cord can be left to hang down at each side of the curtain but a neater finish is created if you use one of the cord tidy devices that are widely available.

INSERTING HOOKS

◆ Carefully even out the gathers or pleats created by pulling up the cords until the upper edge of the curtain looks nice and even from the right side. Insert the curtain hooks through the loops in the tape – you need one curtain hook every 8–10cm (3–4in) – and hang the curtain onto the track or pole. Many heading tapes have rows of loops along them that can be used for the hooks. The row of loops that you use depends on whether or not you want the track or pole to be visible from the room.

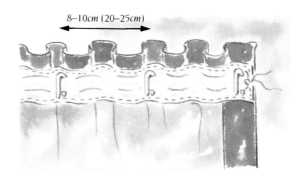

8–10cm (20–25cm)

HEMMING CURTAINS

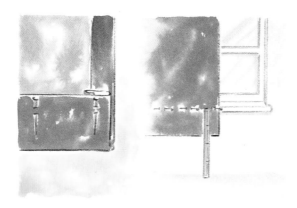

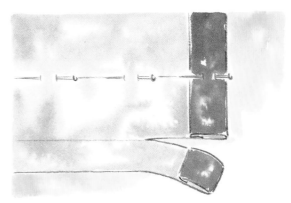

1 ◆ It is a good idea to leave the curtain to hang for at least 24 hours before finishing the hem as the weight of such a large expanse of fabric can make the fabric drop in length. However, if the curtain is resting on the floor or a windowsill it can be a good idea to pin up a rough hem allowance as soon as the curtains are hung to allow the curtains to fall freely and avoid creasing. When you are ready to make the final hem, carefully mark the finished hem line. To ensure that the hem is level, measure up from the floor or windowsill and place a line of pins across the bottom of the curtain at this level. Take down the curtain, taking care not to remove the pins marking the hem lines, and lay the curtain out flat.

2 ◆ Using your chalk and ruler, mark the hem line onto the wrong side of the curtain. Now mark a further line across the curtain the required amount of hem allowance below the first line. For most types of curtains, a hem allowance of 10–12cm (4–4¾in) is adequate. Trim away the excess fabric and fold the hem allowance to the wrong side. Fold under the raw edge and stitch the hem in place in the same·way as the hems along the side edges were made. Press the hem and re-hang your finished curtain.

CHECK IT OUT

*Pastel checks are combined with a pale green
base on these simple unlined curtains to give any room a light
and airy feel without being too feminine. Don't be hesitant about
working with checked fabrics — it is surprisingly easy!*

SIZE

To fit a track 250cm (100in)
long, with finished length of
230cm (92in).

YOU WILL NEED

10.75cm (12yd) fabric,
137cm (54in) wide, with
design repeat of 25cm
(10in)
(see below for how this
amount was worked out)

5.4m (6yd) heading tape

Matching thread

CALCULATING QUANTITIES

These curtains were made to fit a
track 250cm (100in) long, and
their finished length was
designed to be 230cm (92in). The
fabric was 137cm (54in) wide,
with a design repeat of 25cm
(10in). The heading tape chosen
requires double fullness of
curtain fabric.

Taking these measurements,
the ideal finished width of the
pair of curtains is 500cm (200in)

to give the double fullness
required by the heading tape, so
that each curtain has a finished
width of 250cm (100in). As the
fabric was 137cm (54in) wide, two
widths of fabric were needed for
each curtain, making a total of
four widths for the pair. Each
fabric width needed to be 250cm
(100in) long, including a 20cm
(8in) allowance for the top and
hem, so 10m (11¼yd) would be
needed for the four lengths. As
there were four widths needed,
onto this was added three times
the design repeat of 25cm (10in).
So, onto the original 10m
(11¼yd), an extra 75cm (30in)
had to be added, making a total
fabric requirement of
10.75m (12yd).

Each finished curtain was to be
250cm (100in) wide. Allowing
20cm (8in) extra for each curtain
for turnings, 5.4m (6yd) of heading tape was needed for the complete pair.

CUTTING OUT

Checked fabrics are actually very
easy to cut out when making
curtains — you simply follow the
lines of the check!

When making anything from a
checked fabric, it is a good idea to
give some thought to exactly
where the finished hem line will
fall within the check. Always try to
position the hem line so that it
falls at the bottom of the broadest
band of colour. This checked fabric consists of multicoloured pastel stripes running vertically along
each length, with the horizontal
stripes being simple wide bands
of pale and slightly darker green.
Where the two shades of green
meet, there is a contrast peach
line. To give a clean, unbroken
look to the lower edge of the
curtain, the hem line was positioned at the bottom of the darker
band of green but above the
peach stripe.

When working with a checked
fabric, the hem line is probably
more important than where the
checks fall at the top, so it is best
to measure everything from the
bottom upwards! Start by cutting
across the fabric at a generous
hem depth below your chosen
hem line point. Measuring up
from the chosen hem point, mark
where the top of the finished
curtain will fall, add an allowance

needed to be matched. This also meant that the two curtains are not a mirror reflection of each other, but two identical curtains, so that the vertical stripes continue across the closed curtains correctly. In order to do this, it was necessary to trim away a fairly wide band of fabric along the selvedges to be joined.

When joining the lengths for each curtain, ensure that horizontal bands of colour forming the checks match. Pin the two layers of fabric together every 15–20cm (6–8in) or at every focal point of the check – like the peach stripe on these curtains. Place the pins at right angles to the seam line and stitch the seam carefully, sewing slowly over the pins.

Consideration also needs to be given to the positioning of the hem line along the edges of the curtains. As with the lower hem edge, try to position it against a wide band of colour. The finished side edges of these curtains were placed so that they fell just before the next vertical band of colour, leaving a wide band of just the horizontal colours showing.

Normally you would finish the top of the curtain before making the hem but, as the hem point is critical when working with checks, make the hem first and then measure up from here to work out where to fold over the fabric at the top when attaching the heading tape. Any extra allowance should be trimmed away from the upper, not the lower, edge of the curtains to ensure the hem line falls in the correct position.

at the top for attaching the heading tape and then cut across the fabric at this point. This is your first length. Cut the remaining lengths to match this one.

MAKING UP

Follow the instructions given on pages 21–24 for making up the curtains. However, when working with checked fabric, look at the check before starting to sew the lengths of fabric together to see whether it is symmetrical, both in design and its positioning across the fabric width. The check used here is symmetrical but its positioning on the fabric was not – near one selvedge there was a grey/blue stripe while a pink/yellow stripe ran along the other selvedge. To make joining the lengths easier, these curtains were joined midway between the vertical stripes, meaning that only the horizontal bands of colour

LINED, SHEER, LACE & NET CURTAINS

*While unlined curtains are a useful and
easy option for many windows, often you will want your curtains
to be lined, or you may wish to use a sheer or lace fabric
curtain as well.*

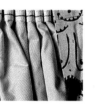

Lining curtains

Curtains are lined for a variety of reasons. The lining adds extra weight to the curtain and makes it hang better. It also helps keep in more warmth and keep out more light, and can also act like double glazing to help keep out noise. Curtain lining extends the life of the curtain by helping to keep the actual curtain fabric clean and avoids any fading that may occur. And, if a similar lining is chosen for various sets of curtains, it creates a more uniform effect to the appearance of the outside of your home.

Curtain linings can be attached to the actual curtain, or they can be made totally detachable. It can save you money if they are detachable as, when you change your curtains, you do not necessarily need to make new linings. Also, the lining – which will have a tendency to need cleaning more often – can be removed and washed easily without the need to clean the actual curtain fabric. If you like to have a heavier curtain for use in winter, the same lining can be used for this set of curtains as well as for the lighter weight pair used in summer.

Curtain lining fabric

Special curtain lining fabric is readily available from fabric stores in a wide variety of shades to match curtain fabrics. Cotton sateen is the most common type of curtain lining fabric and one of the most economical – this is made of pure cotton and has a matt satin-like finish to it. There is also a range of coated curtain lining fabrics available that will help to reflect the heat back into the room. Although these can be more expensive to buy initially, they could save you money on fuel bills in the long run!

Buying lining fabric

It is a good idea to buy the fabric to line the curtain at the same time as the main fabric is purchased. This way you will be able to match the colour accurately and also you will already have the measurements you need to calculate how much to buy! Calculate the amount of lining fabric you will need in exactly the same way as for the main curtain. But remember that you will want the curtain lining to stop short of the actual curtain length – about 3cm (1¼in) shorter is usual – and that your lining fabric may not be the same width as the main fabric. Remember also that you will not need to add extra fabric to match a design as your lining fabric will probably be plain.

Making a fixed curtain lining

There are a variety of different ways in which you can line a curtain. The one given here is a simplified method, based on the one used for unlined curtains, which reduces to a minimum the amount of hand stitching required.

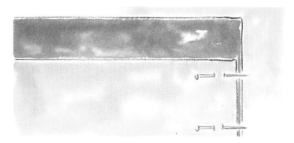

1 ◆ Join together the lengths of fabric – both the outer fabric and the lining – that will go to make up each curtain in the same way as for an unlined curtain (see page 21). Trim away, or snip into, the selvedges and press all the seams open. There is no need to neaten the raw edges as they will be enclosed by the lining. Trim an even amount from both edges of the lining section so that the lining is a total of about 5cm (2in) narrower than the main fabric.

2 ◆ Place the lining and the main fabric sections together, right sides facing, and position the upper edge of the lining below the upper edge of the main section, to allow for attaching the heading tape. Pin the two side edges together, easing in extra fullness along the lining section so that this edge is longer than that of the main fabric. Allow an extra 1cm (⅜in) in the length of the lining for every 90cm (36in) of main fabric.

3 ◆ Stitch the two sections together along the side edges, from the top of the lining section to 20cm (8in) above the lower edge. Press the seam towards the lining and turn the curtain right side out. Fold the edges of the curtain so that the lining seam falls 2cm (¾in) inside the edge and tack (baste) in place. Open out the lining and, from inside the curtain, catch stitch the seam to the main fabric. Press the side edges and lay the curtain flat. Tack (baste) the upper edge of the lining section to the main section across the top, easing in the fullness as you go.

4 ◆ Across the top, fold the required amount of the main fabric over towards the lining. Now attach the heading tape in the same way as for an unlined curtain (see page 22). Remove the tacking (basting), press the edge and insert the curtain hooks. Hang the curtain on the track or pole and leave it for about 24 hours before making the hems.

HEMMING LINED CURTAINS

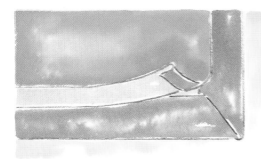 

1 ◆ Linings are best left unattached along the lower edge. If attached with the wrong amount of ease the lining will pull and the curtain will bag out. Mark, trim and then stitch the hem of the outer section as for an unlined curtain (see page 24). At the lower corners, fold in the fabric edge to create a mitred corner effect – this ensures that no raw edges of fabric show once the lining is complete.

2 ◆ Hem the lining section in the same way, ensuring that the lining stops about 3cm (1¼in) above the edge of the main section. As it is highly unlikely that this hem edge will ever be on show, this hem can be machine stitched in place. Once both hems are made, slip stitch the lining in place along the remaining section of the side edges.

MAKING THREAD BARS

 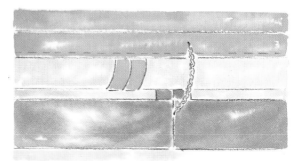

1 ◆ Thread bars help to hold the lining in place, by attaching it to the curtain along the hem edge. Attach a double thread to the inside of the main section along one of the seams and about 5cm (2in) above the hem edge. Make a loop and then pull another loop of thread through this loop. Continue until you have a thread bar about 5cm (2in) long.

2 ◆ Take the thread end through the loop to secure it and then attach this end of the thread bar to the inside of the lining at the corresponding point along this hem edge. Remember that if the main and lining fabrics are of different widths this will probably not be along a seam. Attach the end securely at a point about 1cm (⅜in) above the lining hem.

Detachable curtain linings

Where the curtain lining is totally detachable, you basically have two unlined curtains which hang together, back to back. Each part of the curtain is made in the same way as an unlined curtain – but the lining is attached to a special heading tape designed to make this section easily removable. Have a look in your local hardware store at the range available and check, before attaching the heading tape, that you are attaching it correctly – it is quite likely that the way this tape is attached will vary from the normal way as the lining is often sandwiched between the two layers of the tape. Once the two curtains have been made, they are joined by inserting the curtain hooks through both heading tapes. This makes the lining easily removable for laundering.

Remember to ensure that the lining hem is shorter than that of the outer section. If you wish, you can temporarily attach the two curtain sections together along the side edges with a few stitches. This helps ensure that the lining stays where it should be – out of sight.

Sheer curtains

Sheer curtains are often used together with another pair of curtains in the place of lace or net curtains. They can be made in exactly the same way as an unlined curtain except that, as the fabric is see-through, the seams where the lengths of fabric join need to be stitched in a different way. One way to join the lengths is by making a flat fell seam; another way is by making a french seam.

FLAT FELL SEAM	**FRENCH SEAM**

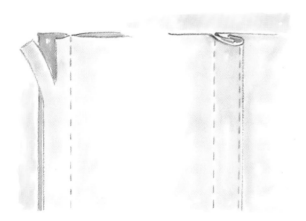

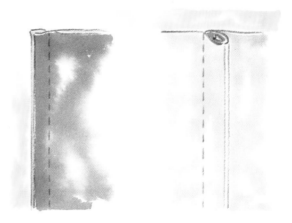

◆ Start by sewing a normal seam, stitching the two sections together with the right sides facing. Decide which side of the seam the flat fell seam is to lie on, and trim away half the seam allowance along the edge at this side. Press the seam so the larger edge covers this trimmed edge. Fold under the visible raw edge so that it encloses the trimmed edge. Stitch in place through all the layers of fabric. A flat fell seam will have a row of stitching visible on the right side that runs parallel to the seam line.

◆ Start by stitching the seam but have the two sections *wrong* sides together and take *half* the actual seam allowance. Press the seam open and then fold the two sections along the seam line with their right sides facing. Now stitch the final seam along the actual seam line, totally enclosing the raw edges. This seam can be pressed to either side.

Lace and net curtains

These are made in the same way as sheer curtains. However, unlike standard curtain fabric which is designed to be hung lengthwise, many lace fabrics are made to be hung widthwise. In these cases you simply choose a lace or net fabric that is as wide as the length of your curtain and buy the amount of fabric needed for the width of your curtain, thereby avoiding the need to join lengths.

Although there is no reason why lace or net curtains cannot be hung from a track or pole, it is very common to find that these are hung from vinyl-coated stretch wires which are hooked into eyelets fixed to the window surround. This is an easy and economical way of hanging curtains that avoids the need for curtain hooks, and makes the curtain very simple to remove for washing.

Start by fixing the eyelet parts of the fixtures into the window frame, ensuring that the stretch wire that will run between them will be exactly horizontal. Measure the length of the curtain by measuring the distance between the stretch wire and the actual hem level of the curtain. Add about 5cm (2in) casing allowance to the upper edge of the curtain and a hem allowance to the lower edge. Many lace curtain fabrics will have a finished edge along one side – this is designed to be the hem edge and you will not, therefore, need to add any hem allowance to these fabrics. On other fabrics a hem allowance of about 5cm (2in) is adequate.

MAKING LACE OR NET CURTAINS

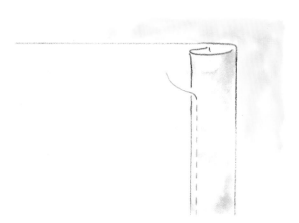

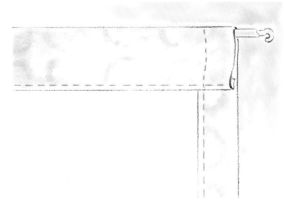

1 ◆ Cut your lace or net fabric to the required depth and ensure that the width of the fabric in the opposite direction is at least 2½ times the length of the wire. Make narrow hems along the side edges by folding 2cm (¾in) to the wrong side. Fold under the raw edge and stitch in place.

2 ◆ Across the upper edge of your lace curtain, fold 5cm (2in) of the fabric to the wrong side. Fold the raw edge under by 1cm (⅜in) to make the casing allowance, and stitch this in place by stitching close to this second folded edge. Carefully insert the stretch wire through this casing, attach the hook fixtures to the ends of the wire and hang the curtain from the eyelets. If your lace curtain fabric has a finished hem edge, you will not need to make a hem. If it does not have a finished edge, mark and make the hem across the lower edge in the usual way.

Lace panels

It is possible to buy complete lace panels to hang at a window. These will usually be finished along all four edges and you will simply need to hang them – usually from a stretch wire slipped through the upper casing or through the 'buttonholes' woven into the top edge.

When choosing your lace panel, take care to make sure you select one that is the correct size. Most lace panels are designed to be hung with virtually one fullness across their width, so select one that is just wider than the window it is to fit. Adjusting the length of a panel can be difficult as it is already finished along all four edges so, where possible, choose a panel the correct length for your window. If you do need to shorten a panel, the extra length should be taken out across the top, not from the bottom where it will be more conspicuous.

FONDANT FANCY

*Bold big prints make stunning curtains –
but involve buying extra fabric to match the pattern. Here, a
cushion and lampshade have been covered using the leftover curtain
fabric. To complete the floral theme, a pretty lace curtain
sits behind the main curtain.*

SIZE

Lace curtain to fit a track
210cm (84in) long with
finished length of 130cm
(52in).

YOU WILL NEED

5.3m (5⅞yd) lace curtaining,
150cm (60in) wide

5.3m (5⅞yd) heading tape

Matching thread

MAIN CURTAINS

These lined curtains were made
following the instructions on
pages 29–30. The fabric used had
quite a large design repeat of
64cm (25½in) and, as four widths
of fabric were needed for the pair,
an allowance of 2m (80in) had to
be made to ensure the pattern
would match. Once the lengths
had been cut, several short pieces
of fabric were left, which would
have been ideal to use for tie-
backs. However, these curtains

are too short to need tie-backs.
So, instead, they were used for the
matching cushion and lampshade.

LACE CURTAIN

This pretty lace curtain was made
following the instructions on page
32. The lace fabric used has a
scalloped edge along one 'selvedge' and came complete with a
finished channel along the other
selvedge, ready to have a stretch
wire slipped through. However, as
the width of the fabric did not
quite match up to the length of
curtain needed, the finished channel was cut off and a heading tape
sewn on instead. The lace curtain
could then be hung on a second
separate track to the main curtains and therefore easily be
drawn to enable the windows to
be opened.

When using a scalloped lace
fabric like this, position the side
edges of the curtain at the highest
point of the hem scallop and
remember to measure the
finished length from the lower
point of the scalloped edge!

CUSHION COVER

This cushion cover uses one of
the flower motifs cut from the
curtain fabric scraps appliquéd
onto silk dupion. Here it is used
on a circular gusseted cushion.

LAMPSHADE

This little lampshade was covered
in two sections following the
instructions on page 67. As the
curtain fabric design is so large,
the floral centres of the design
were used so that an even dis-
tribution of colour and pattern
would be achieved. The inside of
the frame is also lined, in a
matching plain lemon fabric. The
lining was made in the same way
as the outer section, slipped
inside the frame and stitched to
the main section at the top and
bottom. The braid trim covers the
join between the two sections and
the tasselled braid around the
lower edge adds height to the
lampshade and helps conceal
the bulb.

Remember that a lamp with a
fabric-covered lampshade is
highly flammable, so take care!

CURTAIN FINISHING TOUCHES

*While a simple pair of curtains can look
stunning if correctly made, sometimes you may want to add that
special finishing touch to make them look quite unique.*

Curtain tie-backs

Tie-backs are both useful and decorative finishing touches – and are very easy to make. They help to keep the curtains neatly in place when they are open and they can add greatly to the finished appearance of the window.

There is a wide variety of tie-backs you can make. They are usually made from the same fabric as the curtain, often using leftover fabric. Whatever sort of tie-back you choose, they all have a ring at each end that will slip over a hook fastened to the wall at the edge of the curtain. Before you fix the hook in place on the wall, try holding the tie-back around the curtain at various levels until you are happy with the effect it creates. Shaped tie-backs are basically a shaped piece of stiff material covered with fabric. It is possible to buy kits to make these but you can easily make your own at home. The method shown opposite can be used to make curtain tie-backs in any shape.

TIE-BACK WITH CORNERS

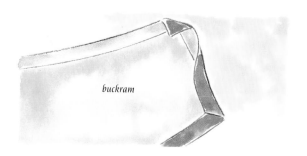

buckram

♦ Mitre the corners of a tie-back so that they lie smoothly. Fold in the fabric diagonally across the corner. Now fold in the edges so that the first folded edges meet. Reduce the bulk by trimming away some fabric beyond the first folded edge.

SCALLOPED TIE-BACK

buckram

♦ For a scalloped tie-back you will need to snip into the fabric to just beyond the edge of the stiffened section so that the fabric will lie flat. Take great care not to snip too far and ensure that the lining section is large enough to cover these cut edges.

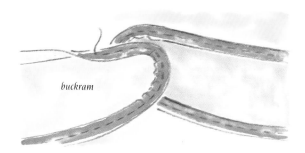

1 ◆ Decide what size and shape your tie-back is to be. Make a paper pattern and hold this around your curtain to make sure it is the correct length to hold the curtain fabric neatly, without it bunching up too much, and that you are happy with the shape. Now cut out this shape from one of the special stiffened materials available for this use, such as buckram. Ask in your local furnishing fabric store to find out what range is available. Now cut out a pair of these shapes from your fabric, allowing extra for seam allowances along all edges.

2 ◆ Lay your stiffened shape onto the wrong side of one fabric shape. Fold the raw edges over the stiffened shape, ensuring that any curves are followed smoothly, and tack (baste) the two sections together. Fold the raw edges to the wrong side around the outside of the second fabric shape, folding in slightly more than the seam allowance and tack (baste) in place. Press both sections from the wrong side, easing in as much fullness as possible along the curves so that the two pieces are as smooth and neat as they can be.

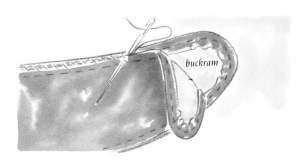

3 ◆ Lay the two sections together with their wrong sides facing. Carefully slip stitch the second lining section in place to the stiffened section and remove all the tacking (basting). Press the nearly finished tie-back from the wrong side.

4 ◆ Securely attach a curtain ring to the lining side of each end of the tie-back. These rings will slip over the hook fixed to the wall. When the curtains are opened, simply loop the tie-back around the curtain and hook the ring at one end of the tie-back over the wall fixture. Remember that when the curtains are closed the tie-back will not be in use – so take care to position this wall hook in such a way that it will be hidden by the edge of the curtain.

Piped tie-backs

Adding a line of piping around the outer edge of a tie-back can create a very sleek effect – but care must be taken when adding the piping.

Measure the outer edge of your tie-back. Cut a piece of piping cord to this length, allowing an extra 5cm (2in) for the join, and cover your cord with fabric as for piping a cushion cover (see page 12).

PIPED TIE-BACK

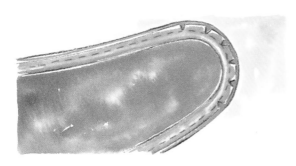

1 ◆ Mark the outline of the finished tie-back onto the right side of one fabric shape and tack (baste) the cord to this shape, matching the edge of the cord to this line. Machine stitch the cord in place with a zip foot attachment on your machine.

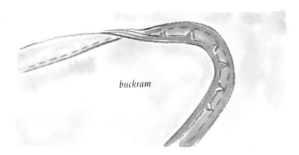

buckram

2 ◆ Lay the stiffened section into this fabric shape, matching the machine-stitched outline to the outer edge of the stiffened shape. Complete the tie-back, slip stitching the lining section in place through the stitched line attaching the piping.

Pelmets and valances

Sometimes you may want either to hide the top of the curtain or to make it a focal point – in both these cases a pelmet or valance is a good idea.

A pelmet is basically a rigid box that is fixed over the top of the curtain, hiding the curtain track. This box can have a shaped front edge and can be made of wood or a stiffened material, such as buckram, that is covered with fabric to match or tone with the curtain. If you choose to make a fabric-covered pelmet, there are kits available for these and, if you have never tried making one before, these are a good starting point.

Valances create a much softer effect and are as easy to make as a curtain. A valance hangs on a second, U-shaped track that sits over the main curtain track. As a valance is basically a second, very short curtain, it is obviously made in exactly the same way as any other curtain and will be easy to remove for laundering.

Swags and tails

These are another way of making a simple pair of curtains look very dramatic and they can often turn the whole window area into the major focal point of the room. Swags and tails are basically lengths of fabric draped across the top of the curtain to form dramatic sweeps of fabric (the swags) and cascading drops of fabric down the sides (the tails). They can be made in many different ways – some of which are very complicated and most of which take surprisingly large amounts of fabric! Depending on the type of swag and tail effect to be achieved, the way in which they are fixed above the curtain will vary. One point almost all swags and tails will have in common is that, to create smooth swags that hang well, the fabric should be cut on the cross – hence the reason why they use so much fabric.

While fully tailored swags are very complicated and time-consuming to make, a very similar effect can be created by simply draping a length of fabric around a second curtain pole that is positioned above the actual curtain. There is no hard and fast rule as to the size of this length of fabric – almost the only way you can calculate the amount of fabric you will require is by cutting a length of spare fabric (such as an old sheet or curtain) and draping this around your curtain pole in several different ways until you are happy with the effect achieved. This fabric can be cut to the desired shape and then used as a pattern for the actual fabric.

While it is best to cut all swags and tails on the bias, it is possible, using this method of draping fabric, to create just as good an effect with the fabric cut on the straight grain – thus greatly reducing the amount of fabric required.

Once the pole that will hold the swags and tails is in position, cut and join a long length of fabric about the same width as your chosen actual fabric and at least four times as long as the pole – this allows sufficient for the swags and to trim the tails to the size you want.

DESIGNING SWAGS & TAILS

1 ◆ Find the centre point of your strip and gently gather up the length to form a soft 'rope'. Position the centre point of your fabric midway along the pole and carefully wind the fabric around the pole, gently easing it into the shape you require. Once you are completely happy with the shape of the swag section wound around the pole, you can start to form the tails. These usually hang to a point about one-third to halfway down the length of the curtain and are cut to create a waterfall effect at the sides. To make this waterfall effect, cut diagonally across the end of the fabric and arrange the tails in neat pleats.

2 ◆ When you are completely happy with your swags and tails, take a few measurements from them and mark certain points on the pole. These marks and measurements will help you to re-create exactly the same effect with your actual fabric. Measure the depth of each swag from the pole and, if you have formed more than one swag, how far apart these swags are. Measure the length of the tails too. Mark points along your pole that correspond to the points where you wound the fabric around it. Once all measurements and marks have been made and you are sure you can re-create this effect, remove the spare fabric from the pole.

♦ Lay your fabric out flat and check that both ends are the same. Now use this fabric to make a pattern for your real fabric, remembering to allow seam allowances along all edges. Swags and tails are almost always lined – this is often done using a contrasting fabric to create a much more dramatic effect but you could line them with the same fabric. Using your 'pattern', cut out and join your real fabric and lining to form this shape. If you are using a fabric with an obvious one-way design, remember that you will need to reverse the fabric at some point so that the two tails are mirror reflections of each other.

Trimming curtains

You may want to trim your curtains for a special finishing touch. Adding contrast sections of fabric to curtains can create stunning effects – and save money. If your curtain fabric is of a width whereby you really need just over a full number of widths of fabric for each curtain, why not make this extra section in a cheaper contrast fabric? In a similar way, a band of contrast fabric can be added across a curtain, perhaps to match a border around the room. Make sure when you choose your contrast fabric that it can be laundered in the same way as the main fabric.

Frills added along the opening edges of a curtain, or across their hems at the bottom, can add a really soft and feminine touch to a room – and, if matched carefully to a frilled valance, will create a totally coordinated effect.

♦ Stitch the main and lining sections together, with their right sides facing, along the entire outer edges, leaving an opening to turn them through. Turn the completed shape through to the right side and stitch the opening closed. Press the edges so that the seams fall along the pressed edges. Following the notes you made from the spare fabric, now wind this final swag and tail fabric around your pole and arrange it to re-create your original effect.

Weighting curtain hems

If you have made a curtain from a fabric that is quite lightweight and it does not seem to hang as well as you would like, add a weighted tape inside the hem allowance. Special weighted tapes are easily available. They consist of a narrow cord filled with little lead weights. Simply buy a length to match the curtain width and slide it inside the hem allowance so that it rests on the hem fold. The extra weight will help to pull the curtain into shape and you will be amazed at just how much better the pleats or gathers will appear once the weighted tape is in place.

It is also a good idea to weight the hems of a sheer curtain with weighted tape if the window it is to cover is often left open – the weighted hem will stop the curtain billowing out into the room every time there is a gust of wind!

STATELY STYLE

*Make your window the dramatic and regal focal point
of the room by adding swags and tails above your curtains!
Extra height was added to the room here by making
the curtains floor-to-ceiling length.*

SIZE

Tie-backs measure 46.5 ×
12cm (18½ × 4½in). Swags
and tails to fit pole 200cm
(80in) long with finished
length of 288cm (115¼in).

YOU WILL NEED

Tie-backs

Leftover curtain fabric

Stiffened material,
eg buckram

Matching thread

Curtain rings

Swags and tails

6.5m (7yd 8in) main fabric,
137cm (54in) wide

1m (40in) contrast print
fabric, 137cm (54in) wide,
for binding

Matching thread

MAIN CURTAINS

These lined curtains were made
following the instructions on
pages 29–30. As the cotton fabric
used was not heavyweight, extra
warmth and weight were added by
the use of a thick, insulated curtain lining. When working with a
printed fabric with as intricate a
design as this, great care must be
taken to match the design perfectly. However much time it takes
you to tack (baste) the lengths
together accurately before they
are stitched will be more than
repaid by the effect created.

The fabric has a fairly large
design repeat and the extra pieces
left were ideal to use for the
matching tie-backs.

VOILE CURTAIN

With such dramatic a print for the
curtains as used here, it would
have been virtually impossible to
find a lace or net that would not
detract from the effect already
created – so choose something
very simple like this voile! The
voile curtain was made following
the instructions for sheer curtains
on page 32. The lengths were
joined using a flat fell seam and
the heading tape used allows the
curtain to be gathered up and
suspended from a rod or stretch
wire. As the fabric is so sheer, to
have simply turned under the raw
edge across the top of the hem
would have left a visible line.
Therefore, to avoid this, the raw
edge was folded down to the
finished hem line, making the
hem an even three thicknesses of
fabric all over.

TIE-BACKS

The simple shaped tie-backs
shown on these curtains were
made from the leftover fabric from
the curtains, following the
instructions on page 37. As the
fabric is such an intricate design,
they were not piped, but simply
stitched around the edge to hold
everything in place.

SWAGS AND TAILS

The dramatic contrasting swags
and tails across the top of these
curtains are created by using an
unlined length of fabric, thereby
greatly reducing the amount of
fabric needed and its weight!
When making a swag from a
single thickness of fabric, choose
one that looks just as good from
both sides as the wrong side of
the fabric is highly likely to show.
The fabric used here is a solid
coloured jacquard weave that

reflects the design of the curtain fabric. To coordinate the look further, it is finished with a wide binding of the same print as used for the curtains. Although both sides of the jacquard fabric are different, they are also very similar, one side being the 'negative' of the other.

Making up

1 ◆ Trim away both selvedges from the main fabric length, and cut the ends straight. Mark points along one long edge 80cm (32in) in from the ends. At one end of the strip, fold the corner in so that the fold runs from the marked point to the opposite corner at that end. Trim away the resulting triangle of fabric along the folded line and discard. Trim the other end in the same way, ensuring that the marked point is along the *same* side of the strip as at the other end.

2 ◆ Fold 2cm (¾in) to the wrong side along the longest edge of the strip, turn under the raw end and stitch in place. Press.

3 ◆ From the print fabric, cut 14cm (5½in) bias strips and join these to form one length of about 9m (10yd). Use this strip to bind the remaining three raw edges of the main section, mitring the corners and having a finished binding width of 5cm (2in). Press.

Hanging the swags and tails

1 ◆ At each end of the finished strip, fold the ends into eight separate sections concertina-fashion to give a 'waterfall' effect to the binding across the ends. Remember that both ends must be done exactly the same, with each fold falling on the same side. Secure these pleats with one or two stitches placed about 100cm (40in) from the very end.

2 ◆ Find the centre of the strip and mark this point along the bound edge with a safety pin.

3 ◆ You are now ready to suspend the swag from the pole – and you will probably need a friend to help! Start by positioning the securing stitches at each end of the strip (above the waterfall tails) on the top at the ends of the pole – have the tail falling behind the pole and, for now, one large drape of fabric falling forwards. Position the tails so that the longest edge falls towards the centre of the pole and make sure the fabric length is not twisted. You may find it easier to hold the tails in place while the swags are draped if they are secured to the curtain pole with drawing pins or panel pins.

4 ◆ Now take the centre of the big drape of fabric under the pole, up through the back and bring it out over the top of the pole to the front again, leaving a fairly tightly wrapped section of fabric around the end sections of the pole and a large drape at the centre.

5 ◆ Wind this drape around the pole again in exactly the same way as before. Arrange the swags so that the safety pin falls midway across the pole and so that everything looks neat and even.

BED COVERS

The addition of a bed cover in a fabric
to complement the other furnishings in a bedroom can create a
very stylish effect without great expense.

The type of bed cover you choose to make is entirely a matter of personal taste – it can be a simple smooth 'sheet' of fabric to match the curtains, or it can be a very complicated patchwork. When deciding what to make, stop and look at the room it is to go in and try to match up some feature already in the room to the style of the bed cover. If you have frill-trimmed curtains, add a frill around your bed cover. If you have a striped wallpaper and printed curtains, mix stripes and prints on the bed cover to link them all together.

Any bed cover needs to fit the bed properly. Therefore, the bed should be measured after it has been made as the extra 'height' added by the pillows and duvet needs to be taken into account. If the bed sits in the room with only the headboard against a wall and there is no footboard, the cover will need to hang over the edge of the bed the same amount along all three visible sides. However, if you have a footboard on the bed, you will not be able to have the cover hanging down along this edge!

Measuring up for a bed cover

Start by deciding exactly how far down the sides of the bed the cover is to hang, and measure the width of the entire bed, allowing this amount at both sides. This will be the finished width of your bed cover. To calculate the finished length of your cover, measure your bed along its length. Remember to measure up and over the pillow area and allow sufficient here to tuck the cover down between the pillows and headboard. If the bed has a footboard, remember to add sufficient here as well to tuck the bed cover in neatly. If the cover is to hang over the end of the bed, it should hang over this edge by the same amount as it extends beyond the side edges.

Simple 'sheet' bed covers

Unless you have a very narrow bed and do not want the cover to hang down at the sides, it is highly unlikely you will be able to make your cover from just one length of fabric – it will not be wide enough!

To work out how many lengths of fabric you will need for the cover, divide the width of your cover by the width of your chosen fabric. Round this number up to the nearest whole number and this is how many lengths of fabric you will need to buy.

To calculate the actual size of each length of fabric, you need to decide exactly how you are going to finish the edges of the cover. If you are going to simply bind the edges, the actual size of these lengths will be the same as the length of the finished cover. However, if you are going to make hems, allowances for these need to be added onto each length. It is possible that you may decide to bind the edges that show, but make a hem across the end where the headboard falls – in this case each length of fabric must match the length of the cover plus a hem allowance at one end only.

Once you know the length of each strip of fabric and how many lengths of fabric you need, you can calculate how much fabric to buy. Remember that if you are using a fabric with a design on it you will need to allow extra fabric to match the pattern. Allow one full pattern repeat extra for each length of fabric over and above the first length – in the same way as you would when making curtains (see page 20).

Before you start to cut out your fabric, decide exactly where the seams are to fall. If your cover requires two widths of fabric and the top section of the bed is just about the same size as one fabric width, the effect will be much better if the second length is cut in half and runs along both sides. The design on the fabric also needs to be taken into account when deciding on the seam positions – try to place the design to create the best effect.

Cut out your fabric lengths and join them to form one large section, remembering to match the pattern correctly. The type of seam you use to join the sections will depend on whether the cover is to be backed or left as a single thickness. If it is to be backed – either by a lining or with quilting – join the sections with an ordinary open seam. However, if the cover is not going to be backed, use a flat fell or french seam to join the lengths (see page 31). Once the lengths have been joined, trim the resulting fabric to the actual size you need for the cover, remembering to allow for hems or turnings.

ROUNDING CORNERS

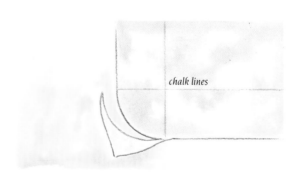

chalk lines

◆ If the cover is to hang down over the corners of the bed it is a good idea to round off these corners so that they do not drag on the floor. To do this, draw lines (with tailor's chalk) onto the wrong side of the cover – position these lines at a distance in from the side and foot edges of the cover that matches the size of the cover overhang. Now draw a quarter circle at the corners and trim away the excess fabric.

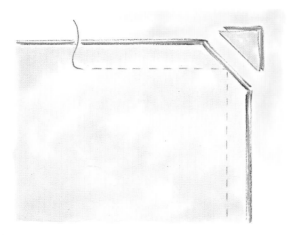 

1 ◆ Cut and join the lining section to match the main section exactly. With their right sides facing, stitch the two sections together along all the outer edges, remembering to leave an opening large enough to turn the cover through. Trim away the turnings at the corners and snip into the seam allowance along any curved edges. Then turn the cover through to the right side.

2 ◆ Press the cover so that the seamed edges fall along the pressed edge and hand stitch the opening closed. To hold the edges neatly in position, it is a good idea to topstitch through all the layers next to the finished edge.

HEMMING AN UNLINED COVER

◆ If the cover is not going to be backed, simply finish the edges in the way you have chosen. Take care when hemming a curved edge that the excess fullness is evenly eased in so that the curve remains smooth. It is often much easier to get a neat finish if the hem along a curve is first tacked (basted) and then pressed before it is stitched.

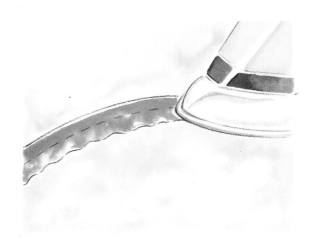

◆ If you have decided to add a frill along the edges of your cover, the main section must be the size of the finished cover minus the frill depth along the edges where the frill is to fall – remember that you will need a seam allowance on these edges. For the frill, cut strips of fabric the depth of the frill plus a seam allowance and a hem allowance. Join the strips to form one long length at least twice as long as the edge it is to be attached to (or three times as long for a better effect). Make the hem along one long edge of the strip and, if the cover is going to be backed, along the ends. Run gathering threads along the other long edge of the frill strip and pin the frill strip to the main section with the right sides facing.

ATTACHING A FRILL

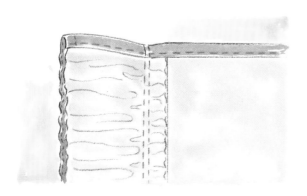 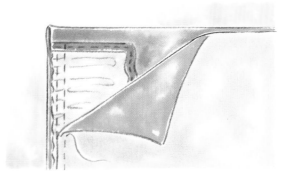

1 ◆ If the cover is not going to be backed, pull up the gathering threads so that the frill matches the edge, positioning the ends of the frill strip level with the ends of the cover. Stitch the pieces together and remove the gathering threads. Finish off the raw edges either by binding them or by neatening them together and press the seam towards the main section. Adding a line of topstitching next to the frill seam will help to keep the frill in place. Complete the cover by making the hem along the remaining edge, continuing across the ends of the frill.

2 ◆ If the cover is going to be lined, pull up the gathering threads to fit the main section, positioning the finished ends of the frill level with the final hem line of the un-frilled edge. Cover the main section and frill with the lining section and stitch all the pieces together, taking care not to catch the frill ends in the seam and leaving an opening in the un-frilled edge to turn the cover through. Complete the cover as you would for one without a frill.

◆ If you are finishing the edges of the cover with a braid, this can be attached to enclose the raw edge. Lay the braid onto the *wrong* side of the cover so that it covers just the hem or seam allowance along the edges where it is to fall. Stitch the braid in place next to the edge and fold the braid back onto the right side of the cover, folding along the seam line. Check that the braid completely covers the raw edge and trim away any extra fabric if you need to. Now stitch the braid in place to the right side of the cover along its other edge, totally enclosing the raw edge.

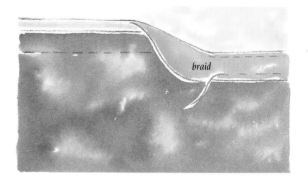

Fitted bed covers

Sometimes you may want to make a bed cover that is fitted exactly to the size and shape of the bed – similar to a gusseted cushion cover (see page 9). To do this you will first need to make a pattern. Measure the top surface of your bed, and then the side sections. Remember to allow for pillows – the depth of the side sections will increase where the pillows are. A fitted bed cover is then made up in the same way as for a 'sheet' bed cover (see page 45).

MAKING A FITTED BED COVER

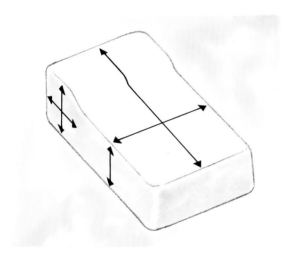

1 ◆ Measure the top flat surface of the bed – this is the main section of your pattern. The size of this section will match the width and length of the top of the bed. At the foot corners of the main section, round off the corners slightly so that the cover will lie better (see page 45). Now work out the size of the side sections. The length of this section must match the length of the edges of the main section that it is to be sewn to. Its depth will be the depth you wish the cover to overhang the edges by. Remember when calculating the depth of the side section that it will probably need to be deeper for a certain length at the end where the pillows are – make your strip widen out at these ends to fit neatly over the pillows while remaining an even distance above the floor. When you have your measurements, make a paper pattern for these sections and calculate how much fabric you will need to buy.

2 ◆ Cut out your fabric and make up your cover in the same way as for a 'sheet' bed cover, joining the side sections to the main section as you would attach a frill. While it is quite possible to create a totally smooth bed cover by simply joining the side section to the main section, you will find that it will be much easier to make a good fitting cover if you allow extra fabric at the corners. Grouping gathers for about 30cm (12in) at the corners will create a soft feminine effect, while a generous box pleat on the corners will give a much more tailored look. Whatever sort of extra fullness you decide to add, remember to allow extra length in the side section for this!

Quilting a bed cover

Whatever shape or size of bed cover you are making, quilting it will improve its warmth and give it a cosy, homely feel. There are many ways of making a quilted cover. You could simply buy a ready quilted fabric and make the cover in the usual way using this fabric. Alternatively you may decide to quilt the cover yourself, perhaps picking out the pattern of the fabric with stitching, or creating your own unique design – or simply joining the layers with lines of stitching.

In order to quilt the bed cover yourself, you will need to buy polyester wadding (batting). Polyester wadding (batting) is readily available in a variety of different thicknesses – choose one that will give the effect you want to create, remembering that once the fabric is stitched to it it may well appear a little thinner. If you are adding a quilting to a bed cover that is already made it will be best to line or back the cover afterwards so that the polyester wadding (batting) is completely enclosed.

MAKING A QUILTED BED COVER

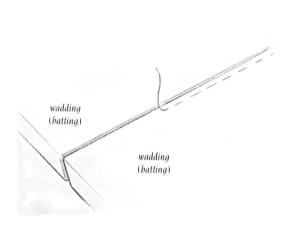

1 ♦ Calculate the amount of wadding (batting) you will need in exactly the same way as you would for the lining section. As wadding (batting) is generally much narrower than most furnishing fabrics, you will need to buy quite a lot! Because of the thickness of wadding (batting), it cannot be joined by making a normal seam as this would create a bulky ridge. It should be joined by butting the edges up to each other and oversewing them securely together – take care though not to pull the stitches so tight as to squash the wadding (batting). If you are using a very thick wadding (batting), trim away part of the edges so that they will overlap and then sew them together – this lessens the risk of the two sections coming apart later, leaving a strip of unquilted cover.

2 ♦ Once you have joined the wadding (batting) to form one large section that is slightly larger than the main section, lay it out flat. Lay the wrong side of the main section over this and check that everything is smooth. Now tack (baste) the two pieces together. It is important to tack (baste) the two sections together over the whole area to avoid any risk of puckering later. Tack (baste) around the outer edges as well and trim away any excess wadding (batting). If you are intending to bind the edges, you can attach the lining now. Turn the whole wadded (batted) section over, cover it with the lining and tack (baste) this fabric section in place in exactly the same way.

If you have decided to make a complicated quilted cover, start by planning out your design on paper. Measure your bed and calculate the finished size of the cover. On a piece of graph paper, draw out the size of your cover and work out the quilting design on this piece of paper, remembering to bear in mind which sections of the cover will fall on the top of the bed and which will hang over the edges. Once you are happy with your design, make your full-size pattern pieces, remembering to allow seams on all the edges to be joined, and calculate your fabric requirements. Cut out your fabric and sew all the sections together to form your one main section. Now cut out and join your lining section.

Once the whole design has been quilted, work a row of machine stitching around the outer edge so that this line will fall just inside the binding or seam allowance. Trim away the wadding (batting) beyond this line of stitching to reduce the bulk and complete the cover in the usual way.

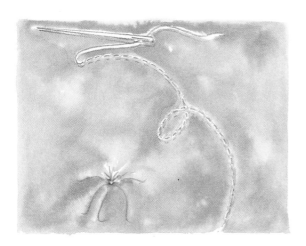

3 ◆ The way the two layers of fabric and the wadding (batting) are held together – quilted – will depend on the design you have chosen, and this can be sewn by hand or machine. If stitching by hand, use a strong sewing thread and work the design using a small running stitch. Pull the stitches up fairly tightly so that the two layers of fabric are drawn together, and remember to fasten off securely. Follow the outline of the fabric design to create an unusual effect or, to make things very simple, simply 'knot' the two layers together. Using a soft embroidery silk, take one small stitch through all the layers, knot the ends together securely on the right side and trim them off to leave a little tassel of threads.

4 ◆ If you decide to quilt the design by machine, work with the main section uppermost. If you are working parallel lines of stitching, each and every line must be sewn in the same direction – if it is not, the quilt will twist and pucker. Start at one edge of the quilt and, as you work towards the other side, roll up the quilt so that it will fit under the machine. If you are following the lines of a design on the quilt, take care to keep the main and lining fabrics smooth as you feed the fabric under the machine foot.

FLOWER BED

Mix appliquéd flowers, quilted strips and patchwork
to create this stylish bedcover.

SIZE

Finished cover is 230cm
(92in) square.

YOU WILL NEED

2.8m (114in) pink fabric,
137cm (54in) wide

2.8m (114in) green fabric,
137cm (54in) wide

1m (40in) yellow fabric,
137cm (54in) wide

Oddment of floral print
fabric from which 9 motifs
can be cut

235cm (94in) square of
fabric for backing

4.4m (5yd) fusible wadding
(batting), 90cm (36in) wide

5m (5¾yd) lightweight
wadding (batting)

Fusible web

Yellow embroidery silk

Matching thread

Making up

1 ♦ From the pink fabric, cut nine
55cm (22in) squares. From the
green fabric, cut 24 strips
measuring 25 × 55cm (10 × 22in).
From the yellow fabric, cut sixteen
25cm (10in) squares. Seam allowances of 2.5cm (1in) are included
throughout.

2 ♦ Apply the fusible web to the
wrong side of the floral fabric
and cut out the nine flower
motifs. Peel away the backing
paper and then apply these motifs
onto the right side of each pink
square. Using a short, narrow
machine zigzag stitch, stitch the
motifs in place, stitching over the
cut edge.

3 ♦ From the wadding (batting),
cut nine 55cm (22in) squares. Lay
one pink appliquéd square onto
one of these squares and tack
(baste) them together along all
four edges. Make up the remaining eight pink squares in the
same way.

4 ♦ From the remaining wadding
(batting), cut sixteen 25cm (10in)
squares. Tack (baste) each of
these squares to the wrong side of
the yellow squares.

5 ♦ From the fusible wadding (batting), cut 24 strips measuring
25 × 55cm (10 × 22in). Apply
each strip to the wrong side of a
green fabric strip.

6 ♦ Working from the fusible
wadding (batting) side, quilt the
green fabric strips following the
zigzag lines showing on the fusible

wadding (batting). Tack (baste)
together along all four edges.

7 ♦ Make up the first narrow panel
that will form the cover. Using
four yellow squares and three
green strips, join them to form
one long strip with a yellow
square at each end. Trim the
wadding (batting) back to the
stitching line and press all seams
open. Make another three panels
in the same way.

8 ♦ Using four green strips and
three pink squares, make the
first wide panel. Join these to
form one long length with a
green strip at each end. Trim the
wadding (batting) back to the
stitching line and press all seams
open. Make another two panels in
the same way.

9 ♦ Join the narrow panels to the
wide panels to create the full
cover, ensuring that the seams
match along the panels. Trim the
wadding (batting) back to the
stitching line and then press the
seams open.

10 ♦ Lay the backing fabric
against the patchwork section
with right sides facing and stitch
together along all four edges,
leaving an opening to turn the
cover through. Trim the wadding
(batting) back to the stitching

line, trim away corners and then turn the cover through to the right side.

11 ◆ Hand stitch the opening closed and press the cover, placing the seam along outer edge. Topstitch close to entire outer edge. Lay the cover flat and, using six strands of embroidery silk and working from the right side, take one small stitch through all layers at the centre of each yellow square. Knot ends securely and trim to 2cm (¾ in) to form a little tuft.

TABLE LINEN

*Lavish dinner parties — and
simple breakfasts — can be so much more stylish if the
table is laid with exquisite linens! And it takes very little time or
effort to create the effect.*

Tablecloths and napkins

These are really easy to make as all you need to do is hem all the edges of one piece of fabric. Measure the table you want the tablecloth to fit, allowing for the cloth to hang down if you want it to, and cut out a piece of fabric this size, allowing for hems along all the edges.

Matching napkins can be made in exactly the same way as the tablecloth by cutting out smaller pieces of the same fabric – the usual size for a napkin is about 45–50cm (18–20in) square when finished. Make sure you cut out the pieces along the straight grain of the fabric and trim away the selvedges.

MITRING CORNERS

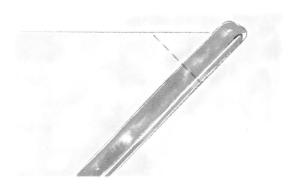

♦ For a really quick and easy tablecloth, make plain machined hems along all the edges. Fold the hem allowance to the wrong side, fold under the raw edge and machine stitch it in place close to the inner folded edge. To make the corners neat, mitre them. Start by folding the raw edge to the wrong side, and then fold the cloth diagonally so that the outer folded edges match. Stitch across the corner, stitching at right angles to the cut edges and starting at the point where the fold touches the finished hem line. Trim away the fabric at the corner, turn the corner through to the right side and complete the hem.

DECORATIVE HEMMING

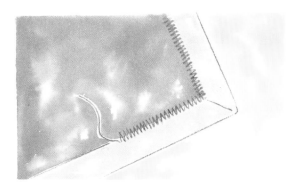

♦ If you want to give your tablecloth an extra special look, stitch the hem in a different way. Make a normal plain hem as you would for a machined hem – but tack (baste) it in place instead of machine stitching, and fold the hem over to the right side. Stitch the hem in place in a variety of ways – try using a machine satin stitch worked over the folded edge, or one of the fancy embroidery stitches your sewing machine can work. Or sew it in place by hand, either with a simple hemming stitch or with a fancy embroidery stitch to make the stitching a focal point.

ATTACHING BIAS BINDING

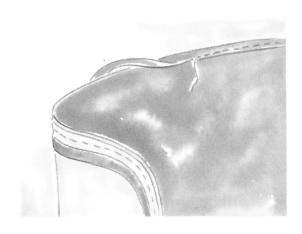

♦ Attaching a bias binding – either purchased or one made of bias cut strips of matching or contrasting fabric – is another quick and easy finish for the tablecloth edges. If the edges are to be completely bound, there is no need to allow a hem along the edges. Matching the raw edges of the binding to the raw edges of the tablecloth, stitch the two together. Fold the binding over the raw edges to enclose them completely and fold under the remaining raw edge of the binding. Stitch this second folded edge of the binding in place. At the corners, fold the binding back on itself so that it creates a mitred effect or trim off the corners to leave smooth curves.

1 ◆ Adding a scallop to the edge of a tablecloth can create a stunning effect. Decide the depth of the scallops and draw yourself a template on a piece of card. Mark on the card two parallel lines – one will be the outer edge of the cloth and the other will be the inner edge of the scallops. Decide how wide you want the scallops and draw curves between the two lines to form the scallops by drawing around a circular object, such as a glass tumbler. Position the glass against the outer line and draw around it, starting at the inner line and continuing around the glass to the next point where it touches the inner line. Move the glass along the line so that it butts up against the end of the first curve and the outer line and draw around it again. Continue until you have a 30cm (12in) strip and then cut out your template.

2 ◆ Lay your template onto the fabric and draw the outline of your scallops onto the fabric – leave a narrow margin of fabric beyond the finished outer edge as this will make it easier to stitch. Position the scallops so that they will match evenly along the entire edge and, if necessary, adjust the size of your cloth to make them fit. Working from the right side of the cloth, stitch around the cloth by machine using a short straight stitch and positioning the stitching just inside the outline, pivoting the stitching at the corners between each scallop.

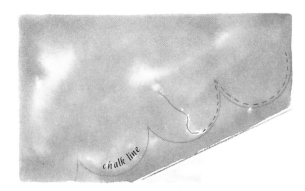

3 ◆ The final scallops can be sewn by hand or machine – but work from the right side. If stitching them by machine, use a narrow machine satin stitch, positioning the stitching over the straight line of stitching. If stitching by hand, use a buttonhole stitch and position the 'knot' of each stitch just over the outline. Once all the stitching is complete, carefully trim away the excess fabric beyond the stitching with small sharp scissors, taking great care not to cut through the stitching.

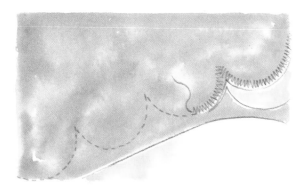

Circular tablecloths

The most difficult aspect of making a circular tablecloth is cutting it out! To work out what size the finished circle of fabric needs to be, add the radius of the table-top to the length of the drop over the edge – this, plus a hem allowance, will be the radius of your tablecloth circle. If you are adding a frill around the edge of the cloth, deduct the depth of this frill from your finished circle.

Your fabric will need to be twice as wide as the radius of the circle if you are to make the tablecloth in one piece. If it is not, you will need to join lengths. When joining fabric for a circular tablecloth it is much better to keep one full fabric width along the centre and to add narrow strips at each side. The seams joining these will be virtually hidden by the folds of the finished tablecloth and the flat table-top area will then remain unspoilt by seams.

CUTTING OUT A CIRCULAR TABLECLOTH

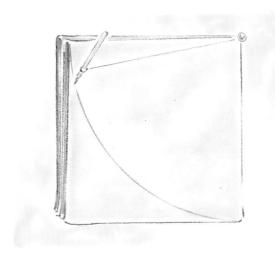

MAKING A ROLLED HEM

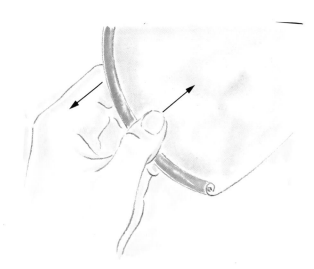

♦ Once you have your square of fabric that is twice the size of the radius of the circle you need, fold it into quarters. Tie a length of string around a pencil and fix a drawing pin onto the string at a distance away from the pencil that matches the radius of your cloth. Position the drawing pin at the centre point of your fabric – the folded corner – and draw a smooth curve onto the fabric with the pencil, keeping the string taut. Remove the string and cut along this pencil line through all four layers – and you should have a perfect circle of the correct size!

♦ The hem of a circular tablecloth can be made in the same way as that of a square tablecloth. However, as the edge is curved, you may find it easier to keep a smooth outline if the hem is tacked (basted) in place and any fullness pressed away before it is finally stitched. If you are using a fine fabric, make a hand-stitched rolled hem. To do this, hold the edge of the fabric between the fingers and thumb of your left hand and gently slide your thumb towards your fingertips, rolling the fabric at the same time. You will find it much easier to grip the fabric and roll the edge if your fingers and thumb are slightly damp. Using a single strand of sewing thread, stitch the rolled edge in place with small, even stitches so that the stitching is virtually invisible.

Place mats

A matching set of table and drink mats will complete the perfect table setting. And, if the mats are quilted or backed with a heat-reflecting or waterproof fabric, they will help to protect your table-top too.

Decide on the finished size of your mat and cut out a piece this size from the main fabric and its backing fabric. If you wish to quilt the fabric for your mats, quilt it before cutting out the shape as lots of closely placed lines of stitching can make the fabric appear to 'shrink'. Quilt your fabric in the same way as for a quilted bed cover (see page 50), using a fairly thin polyester wadding (batting).

The usual way to finish the edges of a place mat is to bind them – so there is no need to add a seam allowance around the outer edges. If you are making square or rectangular mats, rounding off the corners will make it much easier to bind them.

MAKING A TABLEMAT

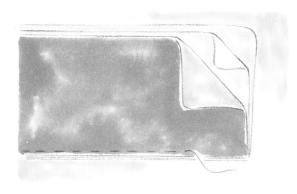

◆ Lay the backing fabric flat with its wrong side uppermost. If the backing fabric is a heat-reflecting fabric, check you have it the right way up – you want to reflect the heat back upwards, not down onto the table. If you are using a waterproof liner, lay this piece of fabric on top of the backing (a piece of shower curtain fabric is ideal). Now lay the main fabric on top of these pieces with the right side uppermost and tack (baste) all the layers together around the outer edges. If you are using a waterproof liner, tack (baste) very close to the edge.

BINDING THE EDGES

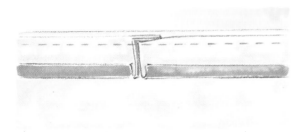

1 ◆ Cut a length of bias binding to fit around the entire outer edge, plus an allowance for joining the ends, and stitch this in place. If using purchased bias binding, unfold one of the folds and, matching the raw edges and with the binding against the wrong side of the mat, stitch the binding to the mat along this un-folded line. Fold one of the ends of the binding to the wrong side so that, when attached, the binding raw ends overlap and are covered. Fold the binding over the edge of the mat so that the other folded edge of the binding just covers the previous stitching line. Pin or tack (baste) in place, then machine stitch around the mat next to this second edge.

2 ◆ If you are making your own bias binding, cut bias strips of fabric four times the finished binding width and join them together to form the required length. If you have a bias tape maker, press the binding to form a strip like that of purchased bias binding and attach it as you would a purchased binding. Alternatively, stitch the binding in place to the wrong side of the mat, matching the cut edges and positioning the stitching line one-quarter of the way across the bias strip. Fold the binding over the edges to the right side, tuck under the remaining raw edge so that the first stitching line is just hidden and then stitch this second edge in place.

FRAMING A MAT

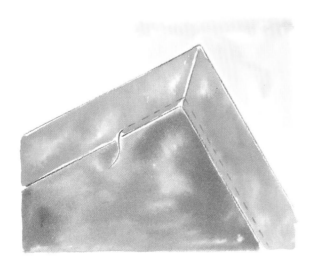

◆ You may prefer to finish the mat with a 'frame' of fabric cut on the straight grain. Cut strips of fabric the width of your frame plus two seam allowances – you need one strip for each edge of the mat. Fold under the seam allowance along one edge of each strip and press. Sew these strips to the edges of the mat, placing the right side of the strip against the wrong side of the mat and stopping each line of stitching at the corner points. Mitre the corners by stitching diagonally across the strips from the finished corner point to the inner edge of the frame. Trim away excess fabric at the corners and press the mitred corners open. Fold the frame over to the right side of the mat, placing the seam along the folded edge. Stitch the inner edge of the frame in place.

STARLIGHT SUPPER

*This elegant table makes the perfect setting for a dinner for two. There is
a tablecloth, quilted place and glass mats and matching napkins.*

SIZE

Finished place mats are
22cm (8¾in) in diameter;
glass mats are 10cm (4in) in
diameter. Finished table-
cloth is approximately
110cm (44in) in diameter.
Each napkin is approx-
imately 50cm (20in) square.

YOU WILL NEED

Matching thread

Place mats and glass mats

30cm (12in) large print main
fabric, 114cm (45in) wide

30cm (12in) smaller print
fabric, 114cm (45in) wide,
for backing and binding

30cm (12in) lightweight
wadding (batting), 90cm
(36in) wide

Tablecloth

1.2m (48in) small print
main fabric, 114cm (45in)
wide

30cm (12in) larger print
fabric, 114cm (45in)
wide, for binding

Napkins

60cm (24in) small print
fabric, 114cm (45in) wide

When selecting fabric for your
tablecloths, mats and napkins,
try mixing colours within the
same pattern range for a coordinated effect.

PLACE MATS AND GLASS MATS

1 ◆ Lay the wadding (batting) out
flat. Cover with the main fabric,
with the fabric right side uppermost, and tack (baste) the two
pieces together all over. Using
tailor's chalk, mark diagonal lines
onto the right side of the fabric in
both directions, positioning lines
approximately 2.5cm (1in) apart.
Stitch the wadding (batting) to
the fabric by stitching through
both layers along all these chalk
lines – stitch all lines in the same
direction or the resulting quilted
fabric will buckle and twist.

2 ◆ Press the quilted fabric, taking
care not to squash the wadding
(batting). From this quilted fabric,
cut two circles 22cm (8¾in) in
diameter for the place mats, and
two circles 10cm (4in) in diameter
for the glass mats. Cut these
pieces again from the backing
fabric. Cut the remaining backing
fabric into 4cm (1½in) wide bias
strips for the binding – you will
need a strip with a total length of
about 2.4m (2¾yd).

3 ◆ Lay one piece of backing fabric
flat with its wrong side uppermost
and lay a corresponding size piece
of quilted fabric on top of this,
with the wadding (batting) side
against the backing fabric. Tack
(baste) the two sections together
around the outer edge.

4 ◆ With the raw edges of the
fabric level and the right side of
the bias binding strip against the
backing fabric, stitch the bias
binding strip to the outer edge of
the mat taking a 1cm (⅜in) seam
and folding under the raw ends to
neaten them.

5 ◆ Fold the binding strip over to
the quilted side and turn under
the remaining raw binding edge
so that the inner folded edge of
the binding just covers the stitching line. Tack (baste) in place.
Stitch in place by machine stitching through all layers just next to
this inner pressed edge. Remove
tacking (basting) and press.

6 ◆ Make the other three mats in
exactly the same way.

TABLECLOTH

1 ◆ Start by cutting the main fabric
into one large circle measuring
112cm (44¾in) in diameter. From
the binding fabric, cut several 5cm
(2in) wide bias strips and join

these together to form one fabric length approximately 3.6m (4yd) long.

2 ◆ Place the right side of the binding strip against the wrong side of the fabric circle and stitch the two together around the entire outer edge, taking 1cm (⅜in) turnings and folding under the raw ends of the binding strip to neaten.

3 ◆ Press the seam open, then press the binding strip onto the right side of the fabric circle, placing the seam along the pressed edge. Fold under the raw edge of the binding to leave a band of binding fabric 3cm (1¼in) wide. Tack (baste) in place, then stitch in place close to this inner folded edge. Press.

NAPKINS

1 ◆ Start by cutting the fabric into two 55cm (22in) squares. Press 6mm (¼in) to the wrong side along all four edges. Now press 2cm (¾in) to the wrong side along all four edges.

2 ◆ Open out the second folded edge and fold the corner of the napkin diagonally, matching the first pressed edges. Starting at the point where the second inner pressed lines cross the diagonal fold, stitch across the corners at right angles to the diagonal fold, ending at the first pressed edge. Trim the corners and turn them through to the right side. Press.

3 ◆ Stitch the hem along all four edges of each napkin by stitching close to the first pressed edge, pivoting the stitching at the mitred corners. Press.

Designer Details

*Here's an opportunity to make all those little extras that give
your home a real designer look. And you may well be looking for
something to make to use up all your leftover fabrics!*

Oven gloves and mitts

Not only are these practical items that every
home should have but, if the fabric they are
made from matches the fabric of your
curtains, they will make it look as though
you have spent a fortune coordinating the interior of
your home. Both oven gloves and mitts are very easy
to make. Oven gloves are made by cutting
out the shape of your hand from layers of
fabric, lining and wadding (batting), then
sewing them together. Oven mitts are made
in one strip with pockets at each end for
your hands. Several layers of fabric, lining and
wadding (batting) are needed to protect your hands.

MAKING OVEN GLOVES

1 ◆ To make the pattern for your oven gloves, simply
lay your hand flat on a piece of paper and draw
roughly around it, allowing a few centimetres (1in)
extra along all the edges. Smooth off the outline until
you are happy with the shape. Cut out this shape
twice from the outer fabric, twice from the lining
fabric and twice from thick wadding (batting). Even if
you are using a quilted fabric, it is a good idea to add
an extra layer of wadding (batting) for protection.

2 ◆ Lay each half of the glove out flat, forming a
sandwich of lining, wadding (batting) and fabric and
remembering to make a pair. Tack (baste) the pieces
together around their outer edges and then bind the
opening edge of each section with bias binding. Now
place the two halves together, with the lining sides
facing, and bind the outer shaped edge. If you wish,
extend the binding at the opening edge and fold it
back on itself to make a hanging loop.

1 ◆ Cut a strip of fabric about 18cm (7¼in) wide and 80cm (32in) long for the main section, and two pieces each measuring 18cm (7¼in) square for the end pieces. Cut all four corners of the main section to form curves, and curve two corners of each end piece to match. Cut all these pieces again from the lining fabric, and then cut the two end pieces again from thick wadding (batting).

2 ◆ Lay the main piece out flat, with its wrong side uppermost, lay the wadding (batting) end pieces onto the ends of this and then cover with the lining section. Tack (baste) everything together around the outer edges, forming a sandwich of lining, wadding (batting) and fabric at the ends. Sandwich together the fabric and lining end pieces and, using bias binding, bind the straight edges of the end pieces. Lay the main sections out flat, with the lining upper-most. Lay the end pieces onto the ends of the main section, with lining facing lining, and tack (baste) all the edges together. Bind the entire outer edge.

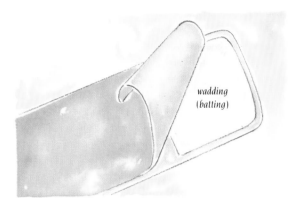

wadding
(batting)

Adding an appliquéd design

Whatever you are making, an appliquéd motif can make all the difference. The way in which this motif is applied will depend on its size, shape and the fabrics being used.

The easiest way to appliqué a motif is to stitch it on by machine, having first applied a bonding web. This bonding web is basically a web of adhesive that can be applied with an iron – like an interfacing. The web will have a paper backing onto which can be drawn the outline of the design. This can be ironed in place to the wrong side of the appliqué motif fabric. The shape is then cut out, the paper removed and this motif then ironed in place in its final position.

Start by choosing your appliqué motif – it can be something traced from a book or one you design yourself. Once you are happy with the design, trace it onto the paper side of the bonding web – remember to reverse the design as you are working on what will eventually be the wrong side of the fabric. Cut out the shape roughly from the bonding web, allowing a small margin around the edges, and apply it to the wrong side of the fabric chosen for the motif. Now cut out the actual motif shape. If you choose to appliqué a motif taken from a printed fabric, there is no need to draw the outline onto the backing paper – simply apply a piece of the bonding web directly behind the motif and cut it out following the fabric design.

Remove the paper backing from the bonding web, place the fabric motif onto the right side of the main fabric in the position you want it, with the right side of both fabrics uppermost, and iron it on.

If you do not want to use a bonding web, apply a lightweight iron-on interfacing to the wrong side of the motif fabric. Cut out the shape and tack (baste) this in place onto the main fabric.

Covering lampshades

Covering a lampshade in a fabric to match those already in the room is a good way to link everything together. Be careful though – do not use a light bulb brighter than 40 watts inside any fabric lampshade and do not leave the light bulb switched on for long periods of time as, unless the shade is treated, it is highly flammable!

ATTACHING APPLIQUED MOTIFS

1 ◆ To attach the appliqué, set up your sewing machine to work a narrow, short zigzag stitch. Working from the right side, stitch around the design so that the stitching covers the raw edge of the motif. Take care to pivot the stitching at any corners and ensure that the raw edge is secured by the stitching along all the curves – any sections left unstitched may start to come free and fray when the item is laundered or in use.

2 ◆ If the motif is a very simple shape, it can be attached with a line of straight stitching. Carefully cut out the motif, leaving a narrow turning around the outer edge. Then fold and tack (baste) this turning in place to the wrong side of the motif. Position the motif onto the fabric it is to be appliquéd to and pin in place. Then stitch it with a line of straight stitching worked just next to the outer pressed edge.

1 ♦ Cover your lampshade frame with cotton tape or bias binding. Although you can use a plain cotton tape, you will find it much easier to get a smooth effect using a bias binding. You can either buy your frame or you can take the cover off one you already have. Wind the tape tightly around all the metal struts of the frame so that no metal is left showing on the parts where the fabric will be attached, and secure the ends with a few stitches.

2 ♦ Lay a piece of fabric against the frame, with its wrong side towards the frame and with the straight grain of the fabric running diagonally across the front of the lampshade. Working slowly and carefully, stretch the fabric to fit the frame, pinning it in place to the tape covering the struts until the frame is covered. If the frame is quite large, use a second piece of fabric for the back, positioning the seams where these two pieces will join along a metal strut.

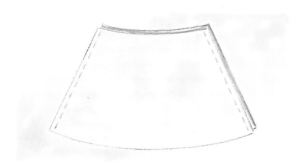

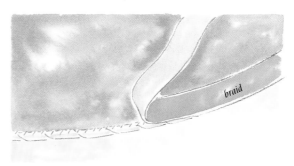

3 ♦ Once everything is pinned in place, trim away the excess fabric, leaving a seam allowance along all edges. Remove the pins holding the fabric to the shade and stitch and press the seams. Use a short stitch length and strong thread as these seams will be under quite a lot of strain when the shade is in place. Fold under the turnings along the top and lower edges and tack (baste) them in place.

4 ♦ Slip the fabric cover back over the frame and pin it in place again. Check everything is smooth and even and then hand stitch it in place to the tape covering the metal frame along the upper and lower edges. Take care to position any seams along the metal struts – otherwise, once the light is on, these will create unsightly shadows down the shade. To finish off the top and bottom edges, attach a braid. Either stitch this neatly in place or glue it on.

RED HOT

*Red may be the colour of danger — but here it
will keep everything in the kitchen safe! Protect your
hands from heat with the oven glove or mitts and keep the
dust off your tray with this tray cloth.*

The oven glove will fit any size hand; the oven mitts are 18 × 80cm (7¼ × 32in); and the tray cloth is 33 × 43cm (13¼ × 17¼in).

YOU WILL NEED

Oven glove

35 × 50cm (14 × 20in) wide striped quilted fabric for outer section

35 × 50cm (14 × 20in) lining fabric

35 × 50cm (14 × 20in) thick wadding (batting)

Oddment of narrow striped fabric for binding

Matching thread

Oven mitts

18 × 80cm (7¼ × 32in) wide striped quilted fabric for outer section

Two 18cm (7¼in) squares thick wadding (batting)

18 × 80cm (7¼in × 32in) narrow striped fabric for lining

Two pieces 18 × 20cm (7¼ × 8in) narrow striped fabric for end sections

Oddment of narrow striped fabric for binding

Matching thread

Tray cloth

35 × 45cm (14 × 18in) wide striped fabric

7 × 160cm (2¾ × 64in) variegated striped fabric

Matching thread

OVEN GLOVE

1 ◆ Make your pattern and complete the oven glove following the instructions given on page 64. The oven glove was bound using 4cm (1½in) wide bias strips of the narrow striped fabric, forming a finished binding width of 1cm (⅜in). You will need to cut and join the strips to form one length of about 130cm (52in).

OVEN MITTS

1 ◆ Make your oven mitts following the instructions given on page 65. The end sections of these mitts are a single layer of fabric – instead of binding the opening edge, fold 2cm (¾in) to the wrong side, turn under the raw edge and stitch in place. The mitts were bound using 4cm (1½in) wide bias strips of the narrow striped fabric, forming a finished binding width of 1cm (⅜in). You will need to cut and join strips to form one length of approximately 2m (2¼yd).

TRAY CLOTH

1 ◆ Cut the strip of variegated striped fabric into four pieces – two 35cm (14in) long and two 45cm (18in) long. Press 1cm (⅜in) to the wrong side along one long edge of each strip.

2 ◆ Lay two strips of different lengths together with their ends and pressed edges matching and right sides facing. Starting at one corner point away from the pressed edges, stitch diagonally across the end. Trim away the excess triangle of fabric and press the seam open to form a mitred corner. Repeat to make the other three mitred corners.

3 ◆ Lay the right side of the mitred corner sections against the wrong side of the large rectangle and stitch together along all four edges. Trim away the corners. Fold the mitred sections over to the right side. Press, placing the seams along the pressed edges. Stitch the inner pressed edges of the mitred section in place.

Suppliers

The following companies kindly supplied materials used in this book. For details of stockists, please write to the individual companies concerned, enclosing a stamped addressed envelope.

G P & J Baker
PO Box 30, West End Road, High Wycombe, Buckinghamshire HP11 2QD
Fabric for appliquéd floral motifs for bed cover (pages 52–3)

Coats Patons Crafts
McMullen Road, Darlington, Co Durham DL1 1YQ
Piping cord and snapper tape for cushions (pages 14–17)

John Lewis Partnership
Oxford Street, London W1A 1EX
Fabric for curtains (pages 34–5), and table linen (pages 60–63)

Liberty of London Prints Limited
313 Merton Road, London SW18 5JS
Fabric for cushions (pags 14–17), and curtains, swags and tie-backs (pages 41–3)

Liberty of Regent Street
Regent Street, London W1R 6AH
Fabric for bed cover (pages 52–3)

Ian Mankin
109 Regents Park Road, Primrose Hill, London NW1 8UR
Fabric for oven glove, mitts and tray cloth (pages 68–9)

Rufflette Limited
Sharston Road, Manchester M22 4TH
Heading tape for curtains (pages 25–7, 34–5 and 41–3)

Stiebel of Nottingham
Abbeyfield Road, Lenton Industrial Estate, Nottingham NG7 2SZ
Fabric for lace curtains (pages 34–5), and voile curtains (pages 41–3)

Vilene Retail
PO Box 3, Greetland, Halifax HX4 8NJ
Wadding (batting) for cushion (pages 34–5), bed cover (pages 52–3), table linen (pages 60–63), and oven glove and mitts (pages 68–9)

INDEX

ACKNOWLEDGEMENTS

The author and publishers would like to thank all those companies who kindly supplied materials used in this book (see page 70).